T0194384

A
Flight Attendant's
DIARY

CLEARED FOR DEPARTURE

K. A. Russell

authorHOUSE®

AuthorHouse™
1663 Liberty Drive
Bloomington, IN 47403
www.authorhouse.com
Phone: 1 (800) 839-8640

Published by AuthorHouse   04/06/2015

ISBN: 978-1-4969-7040-4 (sc)
ISBN: 978-1-4969-7039-8 (e)
ISBN: 978-1-4969-7215-6 (hc)

Library of Congress Control Number: 2015902397

Print information available on the last page.

Any people depicted in stock imagery provided by Thinkstock are models,
and such images are being used for illustrative purposes only.
Certain stock imagery © Thinkstock.

This book is printed on acid-free paper.

Contents

To Daddy

"You are way too happy to be at work." I heard this remark day after day from my passengers. I would always tell them, "This is not work! I was born and raised on a tobacco farm. Now, that's hard work! I enjoy what I am doing, I love people, and I also love serving, so this job suits me perfectly, and I have finally found my niche."

A New Desire

"Are you an airline stewardess when you are not at the bank?"

The question was always the same from clients that came into my office. I always responded the same, "No, why do you ask?" Their answer was always the same, too. "Well, you look like one, and you always wear an airplane pin on the lapel of your suit." I would always explain, "My son is studying at an aeronautical university to become a pilot, so I wear the airplane to honor and support his ambition." But I had to admit, it always left me thinking, "What does an airline stewardess look like anyway?" And besides, me –at my age–an airline stewardess? No way! Impossible! However, the more frequently the question was asked, the more my mind was inclined to entertain the thought. I was enjoying my banking career in my own private office and making a decent salary to boot. I enjoyed my duties and my conversations with my clients daily. Why in the world would I leave this cozy, mind-stimulating career and begin all over again in some area I knew nothing about?

Day after day, there was a stirring within my heart…a new desire and it became more and more frequent. Suddenly, a light bulb came on in my head (kind of like in the movie *Legally Blonde*). I found myself wondering if I should check it out – the reality of being an airline stewardess. Me? No. Change jobs at my age? I had to be out of my mind, but the thoughts became more and more persistent. Hmm, my son was going to be a pilot; my daughter was about to finish high school and would be leaving for college. Why shouldn't I at least check it out?

The thought kept creeping around in my mind, *"My son is going to be working every day at 35,000 feet altitude! Can I trust that? Will my son be safe in his chosen profession? Would I dare?"*

Night after night, I found myself on the computer checking out all the different airlines. Where would I begin? Was there any possibility that an airline would hire me at my age? I applied to all major airlines, and much to my surprise, my age was no problem at all; I learned that employers found people in my age group to be more responsible and dependable employees than those in the younger age group. My age was definitely a plus and I discovered that many others were changing careers at a later age. I was more excited than ever. I was going to join the group!

After sending in my applications, I was shocked that all the airlines accepted me for an interview. I interviewed with most all of the major airlines. Upon being invited to a personal interview, I learned that the airline was going to request that I leave home for 4 to 6 weeks training in their "Hub" location, so I excitedly put in my two-week notice at the bank, and I was off to begin my new second career.

"BOOT CAMP"

At my first commercial airline interview, it was clear that the training would not be a walk in the park. My very extensive training began. You see, becoming an airline stewardess, (which is now referred to as a flight attendant), is not easy to come by. Trainees must make an "A" on every exam for the four-to six-weeks period. Everyone in our group referred to the training as "Barbie boot camp" while we were at the training center.

The trainers gave us a mountain of detailed information, on which we were tested each week while in training. In truth and to my embarrassment, after just three weeks (which was at least half-way through) with the first airline, I made an 88 on an exam, and at that point, I learned another lesson about "boot camp." There were *no* other chances. Without delay, the supervisor hauled me into her office, to give me not only the bad news, but also to hand me an airline ticket to return home – with no job. How humiliating! I had left my banking career, and now I had no job! This was not as easy as one would think. I also came to realize it had been many years since I had studied for an actual exam. Consoling myself, I told myself I was out of practice.

K.A. Russell

Within just a couple of weeks, I accepted an invitation to another airline. Once again, I had to leave home for weeks for the crucial training. I thought to myself, "At least this time, I have an idea of what to expect and I will be just fine."

I was mistaken! Once again, within just three weeks, half way through, I made a score of 89. An almost identical scene took place the second time around. Again, I was embarrassed and humiliated. I was directed into that private office and received the same bad news *and* that free airline ticket to go home!

I cannot fully express my exasperation by this point. I knew the material, but even in school, and all the way through high school and college, I did not test well…you might say I would "freeze up" during exams…exams scared me out of my wits.

I was learning that my dream of becoming a flight attendant was going to take lots of strength and guts. Believe me, it was not just about serving coke and peanuts like most people might think. It's not that at all; it's not all about that pleasant personality either, (although it is certainly a plus). I had heard that statement a million times, and I thought since I had won "Miss Congeniality" in my senior year of high school, it would help – but it did not help me at all!

It's all about the safety of each and every passenger on that plane while it is 30,000+ feet in altitude; it is about knowing how to handle events of medical emergencies, plane turbulence, emergency landings, and an endless list of other potential incidents…so when I say *anything BUT peanuts and coke*, I mean it literally!

So once again, I returned home, without my wings. I began to pray, *Lord, have I made a huge mistake in leaving my job? Do you want me to be a Flight Attendant? Why did you lay this on my heart? You know me well enough to know, when YOU speak to me (at least I thought it was You)...I will not give up. My son is going to be a pilot and I am going to be a flight attendant!* God knew that was the driving force behind my efforts. I was very determined; I wanted to see for myself that my son would be safe at that 30,000-foot altitude every day. So why can't I pull off these 90s on all of my exams? I determined in my heart that day, that with God's help, I was going to make it.

BARBIE BOOT CAMP AGAIN!

After a couple of weeks went by, I contacted a third airline. When I introduced myself, surprisingly, the lady who answered the phone replied excitedly, "Where have you been? (This phone call will forever be etched in my mind.) We've been waiting for you to come to training!" Now, those words stumped me… *they remember me?* It's a very large world. How could they possibly remember everyone they interview? Nonetheless, she had my complete attention and I was totally upfront and honest with her. I very humbly admitted to her the humiliation I had been through at the other airlines.

I will always remember her kind response. She immediately booked me for the next training. (*Oh my, that Barbie boot camp again!*) I would be in their training for six weeks. I graciously accepted her invitation. I've always heard the third time is a charm, and I was going to put it to the test.

I had never been anywhere that far from home. I guess I didn't mention that there was another reason I desired to be a Flight Attendant; it was to see the United States and the rest of the world! This country girl had never been far from North Carolina. Once a year, daddy would take mama, my three brothers and myself to White Lake or Blowing Rock, but only for one day because of all the farm animals and their upkeep. That was our vacation.

BOOKWORM

Upon arrival at training all trainees were sent to the hotel, where we would call home for the next six weeks – away from family and home for most of us. Although it was difficult to be away from my family for such a long period, I was thrilled just to be there. Talk about enthusiasm? I had it; I felt like God was giving me one more shot at my newly desired career.

We arrived at the training center, where there were many trainers and many classes to attend. This time, I decided I was going to get my wings; I was not leaving without those wings I so badly wanted, come hell or high water.

I found myself living with my instruction manual. It was overwhelming – so much to learn, so fast, so quickly. I also enjoyed meeting other students from all over the globe. Wow! I kept thinking, *I am really here.* But I discovered very quickly that I was not going to make the third time around without working even harder than before. Most of the students referred to me as the "bookworm," because every time they saw me, I was camped out in the hall studying our material. I *had* to get my long awaited wings this trip – I just had to! So I decided my study guide was going everywhere I went.

While other students went out to eat in fancy restaurants in the evenings, shopping at the huge local mall, or enjoying a social drink, I was the "book worm" in the hall or in my hotel room with my head in the manual. I "courted" that book; I slept with that book; it was always with me. I was going to make all of the necessary "As" in order to go home with my wings and then begin my new career.

And I was doing it! I was actually making 100s on these exams (about time, right?). If I didn't pull off the 100, it was at least 98; things were looking up. I was going to make it this time. I was beginning to get the idea, God was in this after all and to this day, I am fully convinced He placed me with the company He knew would be a perfect fit for me –I just felt it.

The trainers were excellent, and they were encouraging all along the way. They were team players – and I wanted to be on their team and I desperately wanted them on my team.

One of my classes was the CPR training. I had never had any medical training, but in this valuable class, I learned some very practical medical and life-saving techniques. I thought to myself, *"Wow...this is actually pretty cool,"* as we learned how to check for breathing; how to check the pulse for heartbeat; how to pump on the chest; and how to blow into someone's mouth to give them air. It was an interesting day.

At the end of the day came an announcement that there was a party at the headquarters, and it was mandatory that every class member participate. My first thought was, *"Oh no, I won't get to study this stuff like I usually do,"* but they meant mandatory – so they had a bus/shuttle pick up everyone and take us to the headquarters.

Wow was I impressed. I went to the party, had a diet coke, and then proceeded to dance with some other trainees, just relax a bit, and have a good time.

Suddenly, while dancing, I realized I had turned one of my feet the wrong way – it caused such pain that I had to stop dancing, and continued to hurt so much that I could hardly walk, but I kept thinking to myself, *"It will go away soon; it will be ok. I am in training; it just **has** to go away."*

As the party ended and everyone was leaving, I headed to my shuttle, still limping like a hurt puppy. I kept assuring myself it would soon pass. The shuttle took us back to our hotels for the evening. The weekend was ahead of us and lucky for me there were no classes for the next day.

THE NUTTY BUDDY

That evening, right in the middle of my studying, for some strange reason I was craving ice cream - I just had to have a nutty buddy...remember those? I still can't explain why that idea just popped into my head, but I knew I had to get one, and continue my studying.

By this time, my foot was very swollen and had begun turning black and blue; however, the thought of that nutty buddy trumped the hurt, and I slowly limped down the long hall from my room to the gift shop to get that much-wanted treat.

As I was checking out to pay for it, the cashier noticed my foot, which was really looking awful by that time. "Honey, don't you know you are walking around on a broken foot?"

I immediately responded, "No ma'am, I just sprained it today... it turned the wrong way."

She responded, "I know what I am looking at, and you most definitely have a broken foot!"

"No – I am at training to become a flight attendant, and I cannot have a broken foot! It's just a bad sprain," I insisted.

"Well, I've had a broken foot before, and I am telling you one more time, you need to see a doctor and get an x-ray. I know what a broken foot looks like."

I tried to be courteous, but my patience was wearing thin by that time, and I was becoming annoyed. "Thank you very much, but my foot ain't broken! See? I am walking on it…besides, like I said, I am at training to become a flight attendant, and I simply can**not have** a broken foot!"

I thanked her for the nutty buddy and then limped out of the gift store – to enjoy my treat.

I hopped up the long hall with my nutty buddy in hand. All of a sudden, my foot began throbbing; the pain really kicked in and then something totally unforeseen happened: I fainted! Right there, I passed out from the pain. Of course, I didn't realize I had passed out…until…I heard voices… they were discussing someone. That someone was *me*. I heard everything they said but I could not respond.

"Is she breathing? Do you get a heartbeat? We need to pump on her chest and blow into her mouth!

Those are the words I heard…then I remember thinking to myself, "*Man, you better **not** pump on my chest! And you better **not** blow in my mouth! I am not dead!*" Finally, I was able to open my eyes. Standing over me was a crowd of faces. They were the students from my class that day, both guys and girls. They were leaning over me whispering, "She passed out! Do something!"

I believe that is when I was finally able to speak – because my only words were, "Hey, I am okay – you better not pump on my chest or blow in my mouth. I am alive."

They sat me up, checked my vitals…then the questions: "What happened? Are you alright? Why did you pass out? You need to go to the ER."

I argued with what little strength I had. "No, I am not going to the ER – don't you get it? I am in training; I ain't leaving this hotel – I am alright. I cannot go to the ER, the trainers might send me home – and I am here to get my wings."

Then two really nice guys from my class picked me up off the floor, and literally carried me to my room. To this day, I do not have any idea what happened to that nutty buddy I just had to have. All I remember is waking up to many faces bending over me. These guys were super nice; they got me back to my room. I limped in and stayed there the remainder of the night, while studying my book and watching my foot swell in size and turn multiple shades of black and blue.

The next day, thank the Lord, we did not have class, but everyone who witnessed my passing out came by my room to check on me. They even noticed my foot was worse – much worse. Some of the students actually lived there, and one of them offered to drive me to the nearest ER to get an x-ray. At first, I refused. But about half way through the day, the pain became so intense, that I accepted the invitation to drive me to the ER.

In my narrow mind, I was thinking, "*I am so far away from home. I am in training to become a flight attendant. All I want to do is to Get My Wings and graduate as a flight attendant (this time)!*" That was all I wanted to do, for heaven's sake. However, those nice friends insisted they drive me to the ER. The doctor took one look and immediately ordered an x-ray.

"Well, it looks like you have a broken foot, but we will be sure with the x-ray." I did not want to hear those words. The x-ray proved the doctor was correct (as well as that cashier I had argued with). My foot was indeed broken. They placed my foot and my leg in a cast all the way up to my knee and put me on crutches.

Can you believe this? This time I was finally making all A's – half-way through training and all I lacked was three more weeks, and there I was on crutches? Unbelievable!

"I'm Not Going Home"

The following morning, the hotel phone beside my bed rang. I answered it out of curiosity. Who in the world would be calling my hotel room? I kept in touch with my children and mother while away from home on my cell phone. I answered to find myself speaking to one of the supervisors.

"Are you alright?" she asked.

"Yes ma'am."

"Did you have to go the hospital yesterday?"

"Yes ma'am," (wondering *how she knew).*

She wanted to know if I was indeed ok and what had happened. That is when I began to cry softly while responding to her questions.

"Ma'am, I kind of hurt my foot at the party, but I promise you it is okay now. Are you going to send me somewhere?"

"Where would I send you honey?" That's when the tears really started flowing.

"Home…are you going to send me home because I hurt my foot? I can still come to class, and I will be there tomorrow. But if you are thinking about sending me home, I don't want to go – please, I want to stay and get my wings."

"If you are okay and can make it to class, of course we are not going to send you home." The chuckle in her voice sounded like angels singing.

"Thank you! I will see you in class!" I was so relieved.

On crutches, the next day I happily made my way to the shuttle bus to take us back to the training center. The next several classes, I realized the difficulty of handling all of the paperwork and our workbook, while holding on to my crutches. One of the nice guys who had carried me back to my bedroom the evening I fainted came over to me and offered to carry my books and purse to and from each class. Bless his heart…what a gem of a guy! I couldn't have made it without his help as well as help from the other classmates.

One morning, I hopped into one of the medical training classes. It appeared that only the trainer and I were present. She took one look at me hopping in on crutches and said, "Good morning," with a puzzled look on her face. I returned her greeting with a faint smile.

"Ann, do you actually think you can perform CPR on the dummy on the floor with those crutches?"

"Yes I can, ma'am, I can – you just watch me." I parked my crutches along the wall, got down on my knees on that floor, where I proceeded to perform the necessary CPR. She stood and watched me in total amazement.

"Good job!"

I got up and retrieved my crutches, "Thank you! I knew I could do it!" I exclaimed.

Thank the Lord, by this time, we were in the final weeks of training, with only one week to go, and then the big day of the final testing. All of the trainers and students in my classes made a special effort to be helpful to me throughout the remainder of our time in training. And to top things off, I was still making the necessary "A," mostly 100s – and oh boy, was I ever thankful and grateful! I was beginning to see the end of this long-awaited journey.

Amazingly, and only through the grace of God, I managed to get through the remainder of the training without a hitch. Thankfully, we had already performed emergency evacuations from the plane before my broken foot, which I considered another gift from the Almighty.

The day arrived for our final testing. I remember vividly calling mother and daddy and my children with the excellent news!

"I Made It!"

They were ecstatic! And the best news of all; I was going home! After being away from my loving family and going through a lot of very intense hard work, I left for North Carolina *with wings* pinned to my lapel, and I was proud to be an employee of the Airlines. I was one happy country girl with my accomplishment.

The Airlines took a graduating class picture of everyone that day. I had to sit on the front row on the floor in shorts, sporting the cast on my leg and foot. I believe they told me I was the first class member to ever graduate on crutches and in a cast. They had no idea of the pride I felt within, even with that cast on my leg. I was ever so thankful finally to have a job that I had so much wanted. I was also equally proud to be with the Airline I felt God Himself had hand-placed me – exactly where He wanted me to be – with the company He planned.

However, I still had four to six more weeks of recovery at home. So instead of beginning to work flights like all the other students did the day after our pinning of the wings, I had to be flown directly back to North Carolina for rest and recovery. Though sad that I didn't get to perform my duties as a brand new Flight Attendant on the same day as my classmates, I was thankful and ready to go home for the much-needed foot healing for the next few weeks.

9/11

Upon arrival home, I stayed on the living room sofa, with my broken foot propped up on a chair, anxiously waiting for healing. All I could think about was beginning my new career. I could hardly wait!

On my second day home, around 9:00 a.m., the phone rang; it was my mother.

"Ann, did you see that pilot fly his plane into a building in New York?"

"No Mother, and no pilot would do such a thing," I replied. "Why do you ask?"

"You may want to turn on Fox News," mother responded.

I immediately did what she asked. I was in shock and stunned as I saw the sad news of the World Trade Center burning, knowing that all the people on the plane had died and thousands of people in the building were probably doomed. I continued to watch in despair as the entire building crumbled to the ground. This horrible event happened just three days after my graduation from training.

Mother was still on the line, and we watched in total disbelief together as the other plane crashed into the second building. "Ann, are you absolutely sure you want to go back to the airline and be a flight attendant? Are you sure? It doesn't look very safe."

"Mother, Brad is still going to be a pilot, so absolutely, I will continue with my new career." I also reminded her how difficult it was for me to get the job, adding, "Yes, mother, I will return once my foot is healed."

I called my son, Brad, to see if he had seen the news. Of course, we continued to stay in touch throughout the remainder of the day. My question to him was the very same question my mother had asked me.

"Son, are you positively certain you still want to be a pilot? Are you absolutely sure?"

His response was the same as mine, "Yes, mama. I am here to study to become a pilot, and I am not pulling the plug now."

I responded, "Well, okay, if you are going ahead with it, so am I."

Then some of my classmates and friends from my graduation class began contacting me by cell phone. They were all scattered across the United States. They were away from home for days, because everything stopped on a dime. All planes were grounded; thus, the flight attendants ended up spending as long as a week away from their homes. They were all scared and filled with uncertainty to say the least. But they were all safe. They all assured me they were still going to continue flying – it hadn't changed their minds either.

THE SAMPLE

After several trips to the doctor, he finally released me to begin my new career. I was still slightly limping because the foot was still healing, but I was anxious to begin, the sooner, the better.

I graduated on September 9, 2001, but because of the broken foot, I actually began my first flight on October 10, 2001. My first "home base" was Chicago. I had never been to Chicago, so this was exciting to me. Sporting my new uniform and my wings, I made my way from Raleigh-Durham (RDU) to Chicago. Before I could work a complete trip, it was mandatory that all new employees start their flying career with their first day at work on the plane for an entire day, working with other crew-members, who were actually working their trip. This better equipped us, as it gave each new flight attendant a good idea of the real thing. I was able to observe their duties all day, which was both exciting and educational.

As you will soon see, that first day would remain etched in my memory for the rest of my life. I was given the good fortune to work with an airline crew from Chicago Midway Airport; they all had been with the airline for years. While I was very busy, trying to do everything to perfection, the head crew-member, who happened to have twenty years of working as a flight attendant under his belt, was there to have a good 'ole time with a country girl from North Carolina. It must have been stamped on my forehead or something, because this gem of a guy had a bag of tricks under his hat, and I believe he used all of them on me that day!

Every time the plane landed, I was very busy crossing every seat belt on each seat, and made sure I placed them accurately and perfectly. After his observation of my attention to detail, he pulled me over to the side while we were flying, and sweetly said, "Honey, you are knocking yourself out! As long as the seats are clean from trash, and the seat belts are in the seats where the passenger can easily sit down and buckle up, the job is done. Stop wearing yourself out. Just breathe! We're glad to have you – so just enjoy your first day!"

I tried to do what he suggested, but he didn't know the full extent of my hard work to get there, and I so wanted to get it right.

That day, one of our stops was New Orleans. Of course, I had never been to New Orleans. "Have you ever had a 'beignet?'" he asked.

"What is a 'beignet?'" I replied.

"Then you haven't ever had one; I am going to get off the plane and grab a few for all of us," he said with an excited voice.

I thought to myself, *"Wow, this guy is really nice, and he is doing all he can to put me at ease."*

Sure enough, he returned later, paper bag in hand, with my very first beignet.

"Eat and enjoy – on me!" he said.

But I noticed we were beginning to board our new passengers and the first day on the job, I did not want the passengers to see me eating. I shared that with him, as he was eager to know how I liked it.

"Okay," he replied. "Just save it for your hotel room tonight. I hope you enjoy it."

During the next flight, all of the flight attendants came to the back to pay me a visit after we had finished our first round of service and picking up the trash. They were discussing the fact that an FAA inspector was going to meet us on the ground at our next landing, and that we all had to have a "sample" ready for the inspector.

"A sample of what?" I asked.

The head crew-member said, "You know… a sample."

"Are they going to put a needle in our arm to draw our blood?" I innocently asked.

They were all grinning, and he said, "No honey, they just want a sample."

I still didn't get it.

"Exactly what do they need a sample of?"

"Urine," he replied.

Well, that got my undivided attention. "What? A urine sample? Right here on the plane? What will we put it in? We are not in a doctor's office; we do not have anything sanitized. What on earth is this all about and why does he need a sample of our urine?" By this time, they were all hiding their laugh, but I was still clueless.

Then he said, "Sure we have something to put it in. Use one of our small clear plastic cups."

"But they are not for that purpose," I argued. "And besides, how can we keep it from spilling? What can we use as a top? Those cups do not have lids."

"You know that little top that we use for straws for the children...just use that," he explained.

"But it has a hole in it," I replied.

They all reassured me that it would be perfectly okay to do it in the little cup. "Where are we supposed to store it until we land?" I asked.

"Just drape a napkin over it, and hide it away in the cabinet in the lavatory under the sink. That way, none of the passengers will find it when they use the restroom," he answered with a straight face.

I grumbled, "I just don't understand this! I don't get this at all! And to think I left a good position at the bank in mortgage loans, and now you are asking me to urinate in a plastic cup on this plane! I just don't get it!"

So we continued with our drink service and gathering the trash. In the meantime, while I was alone in the galley in the back of the plane, I proceeded to do exactly as I had been instructed. I got one of the cups with a lid, went into the lavatory and put a tiny bit of my "sample" in the cup, and carefully placed the lid on it securely. Then I wrapped a napkin around it and placed it under the sink, according to instructions.

During this ordeal, I was thinking, *"Man! This is really strange! Why don't the airline FAA inspectors get these samples in an office somewhere? Why on this plane?"* Okay, whatever it took…I figured it was all part of the job and went about my duties.

Shortly afterward, one of the female flight attendants came to the back to visit me. She asked, "Do you have your specimen ready yet?"

I grumbled under my breath, "Yes, I do."

She asked, "Where is it?"

I responded, "In the lavatory, under the sink, just like *he* told me to do. I just don't get it! I can't believe they are taking our specimens right here on this plane," I continued to object.

Then she told me the most disgusting thing I had ever heard in my life. "Well, *he* is so upset that the FAA inspectors demanded our specimens while we are on duty, he actually put a little something extra in his."

"What do you mean? What something extra did he put in it?"

"A little poop," she responded.

"What! No way! No he did ***not***!" I could not believe what she told me.

Shortly, the head crew-member came down the aisle, carrying his cup with a napkin draped over it. Then he showed it off to all of us! He had really done it – in the cup! This was so embarrassing to me! I couldn't believe my eyes! But there it was, big as life!

"I can't believe you did that! How gross!" I shamed him.

In looking back, I wish I could have seen my face throughout this ordeal. Only my crew-members witnessed my expressions. I can tell you, coming from the country, this was unspeakable stuff going on. But I was not going to let a sample specimen jeopardize my job I had worked so hard to get, so I complied.

He instructed me, that when we landed and after the passengers had gotten off the plane, for me to come to the front of the plane with my cup. I again, grumbled, but I agreed.

WHERE IS THE **FAA?**

After that rather long flight, we finally landed. When all the passengers had deplaned, I proceeded to retrieve my cup from the lavatory, just as I had been instructed and made my way down the aisle to the front of the plane.

There stood all three crew-members and myself, with cups in hand. But there was a strange conversation going on. They seemed to be confused. They were trying very hard to decide whose cup belonged to whom. I had to ask, "What are you all discussing?"

"We are trying to figure out who each cup belongs to, besides mine, which is very clearly mine," the really nice guy replied with an impish grin.

"What?" I asked. "You guys didn't put your names on the cups?"

"That's it…there is no way to identify the owner of each cup. He said, "I guess I will have to smell each one."

"My word!" I exclaimed. "Man, don't you know urine is urine? All urine smells the same! Are you out of your mind?"

"Oh, you are right. Then, the only thing I can do is taste it to see who belongs to each cup."

"What! You are actually going to taste this stuff? Are you crazy?"

"Well, that's the only way we can know for sure who belongs to each cup, I think." Then he proceeded to do just that – he literally tasted each cup, including his own! I was in total disbelief.

"What have I gotten myself into? This is the grossest thing I have ever witnessed in all my life! And by the way, where in the world is that FAA inspector?" I was thinking to myself.

By this time, all of the three crew-members had tears streaming down their cheeks. "What in the world do you possibly find funny here?" I screamed.

They were rolling in the aisle laughing. (I forgot to mention that all this time, there were actually a few "through" passengers on board, perhaps five or six. They also were enjoying the conversation.)

"What is so dog-gone funny? And where is that dang FAA inspector?" I was getting a little aggravated.

That is when the "really nice guy," the one with those twenty years under his belt, put the cup down on the counter. He placed his arm around my shoulder and exclaimed. "Honey, you are a **real** team player! Welcome to the Airline! And, Honey, you get an A+ for sportsmanship!"

I still didn't get it. "What do you mean?" I asked.

"It was not urine in our cups at all – it was apple juice!"

And the other stuff in his cup? It was part of a candy bar! I stood there, relieved that he had not tasted anyone's urine after all! Then the reality of what just happened hit me ... I had been duped!

"Am I the only one on this plane who actually tinkled in this cup?" I asked.

Overwhelming laughter filled the plane. Then the "really nice guy" said, "Yes honey, and you did it beautifully! One thing we know for sure, you surely do know how to follow instructions to the **T**! You are going to make the best flight attendant ever! We are so happy to have you aboard our Airline and part of our crew!"

The through passengers were still laughing after it was over. The flight attendants apparently had told them previously what was going to happen, and what to expect from the "new girl" on the plane. They too, welcomed me aboard.

As for me, I tried to react like a proper Southern lady, who knew how to take a joke. I was doing my best to get through my first day on this new job as a flight attendant. But I was very thankful that the FAA inspector never showed up! What a relief for a brand new attendant.

That "nice guy" was a real trickster – all day long. He continued to pull other tricks as well as this one, which I will remember to my grave. At the end of the day, I grabbed my luggage, and the paper bag containing that "beignet" to take with me to my hotel room my first night in Chicago.

You have just heard the story of my very first day at work on the plane, and what a day it was. Little did I know it was just the beginning of many unforgettable days that lay ahead.

THE BEIGNET AND AN EMERGENCY CALL

That evening, we landed back at Chicago Midway, where we had begun early that morning. That meant we were "finished" with work for the day. I thanked all of them for helping me, and for their idea of "fun," promising all of them that it was a day I would never forget. They assured me I did a great job and wished me great days ahead in my new adventure. What a day it had been! Little did I know that there was more action to come!

I made my way back to the employee lounge in Chicago and then took a taxi to a hotel for the night. It was my first night away from home in a different city. I cannot deny there was a little fear in anticipating the adventures that lay ahead of me in my newly acquired position. I was no longer at home every night with my kids, as I was accustomed, and I was no longer in my own home and my own bed. I don't think all of those things hit me until I found myself alone in that hotel room for the night, while I was getting ready for my trip the next day.

After calling my family, you have to know the first thing I did upon arrival in my hotel room. Yes! I had to try that long-awaited beignet. I was to discover beignets are commonly known in New Orleans. It is an English "fritter," which is the French term for pastry made from deep fried choux pastry, covered with powdered sugar. It was very sweet and tasty. I happen to have a sweet tooth, so it hit the spot.

After finishing my treat, I threw the bag in the trashcan, along with my plastic gloves from my pockets in my uniform. During one of the landings, I was so busy cleaning the plane and perfectly placing those seat belts in each seat, that I didn't have time to take off my gloves and toss them in the garbage, so I had stuffed them into one of my pockets. I had forgotten all about those gloves, probably because of those darn tricks they played on me.

I had to press my uniform before bed, so it would be ready first thing the next morning when I would begin my very first three-day trip. I set my alarm and went to bed. I could hardly sleep for the excitement.

The following morning, I showered, dressed and checked out of the Chicago hotel, and took a taxi back to the airport to report for duty. I was very nervous but very thankful for my new job. I wasted no time getting to the airport. I went straight to the employee lounge to check in for my first three-day trip, and waited there to meet the other two crew-members.

While waiting in the employee lounge, my cell phone rang. It was Crystal, my daughter. She said, "Hey mama, we miss you! But we know you are excited to be there on your new job, and we are all so proud of you!"

"Oh, honey, I miss you, too. I love you."

"Mama, some strange woman just called my cell phone. She said she was the hotel manager there in Chicago. She was asking for your cell phone number. She said you put down my number in case of emergencies, and there is an emergency."

"What kind of emergency?" I asked.

Crystal responded, "I don't know mama, but she wants you to call her right back. She said it was urgent you contact her immediately."

Crystal gave me the number, and I anxiously returned her call. The lady who answered that phone number asked, "Are you Karen Ann Russell?"

"Yes ma'am, this is Karen," I replied.

"I am the manager at the hotel in Chicago where you stayed last night. You did stay at our hotel, am I correct?"

"Yes ma'am. Why are you calling me?"

"Ms. Russell, our maid found something in your room while she was cleaning. You have to be very honest with me, because I am going to put the Chief of Police on this phone call in a moment for a conference call."

I was stunned, "Ma'am, what on earth is the problem?"

"Ms. Russell, the hotel maid found a white powdery substance along with a pair of latex gloves in your trash can. Can you identify these items for me? What were you doing with the white powder and latex gloves in our hotel last night?"

"Ma'am, it's nothing to worry about," I assured her.

She then got very annoyed with me. She accused me of being very relaxed over such a topic.

I said, "But please taste the white powder. It's nothing but powdered sugar."

"How dare you!" She screamed. "This is important business! You are violating the law! I will have you arrested immediately if you do not tell me what this substance is!"

By this time, all of the other flight attendants in the employee lounge (about 75 people) could not help from hearing my conversation, because all of them grew quiet. You could have heard a pin drop. Everyone was looking at me! The New girl. What has she done?

I continued to explain to the lady, "Ma'am, really, if you will just taste it, you will see that it is the powdered sugar from a beignet that I ate last night."

In a very angry voice she asked, "What in the world is a beignet? I am going to contact the Chief of Police in Chicago if you don't get straight with me!"

I began stammering – because I suddenly realized this lady did not believe me. I tried explaining, "Ma'am, I am a new flight attendant. Yesterday we flew through New Orleans, and a fellow attendant bought me a beignet to celebrate my first day; I didn't have time to eat it on the plane, so I ate it in my hotel room last night. It's just powdered sugar and my gloves from the plane. I put them in my pocket yesterday between flights, because I forgot to put them in the garbage before getting off the plane. Why is this such a big deal?"

She then added, "You don't know what the **big deal** is?"

"I'm sorry, ma'am, but I do not," I answered truthfully.

Suddenly, our two-way conversation became a three-way conversation. I heard a man join in on the phone call. He was the Chief of Police in Chicago, and I was in very big trouble! I thought to myself, *"Aw man, I have worked so very hard to get here - my first day as a real flight attendant and now this? I am not believing this! God, please help me."*

Then the man began by saying, "Ms. Russell, what are you confessing to here?" I said, "Sir, I'm not confessing to anything. There is nothing to confess. I haven't done anything wrong!" By then, I was in tears. All eyes were on me in the employee lounge, and they were watching suspiciously and listening carefully to my every word.

"Sir, as I explained to the hotel manager, it is just white powdered sugar from a beignet that a flight attendant friend got for me yesterday when we flew through New Orleans! Why are you getting so upset over this? I do not understand!"

"Ms. Russell, are you not aware of anthrax?" he asked.

"Yes Sir, but what does that have to do with me or my beignet?"

"It is against the law to possess anthrax!" he answered.

"But sir," I pleaded, "I have never possessed any anthrax. I have never touched any type of drugs. You have to believe me."

About that time, a police officer walked into the employee lounge, alongside the airport manager. They came in announcing, "Is there a Karen Ann Russell present?"

I was still on the phone begging my way out of that horrible mess, crying, my knees were knocking, and I ever so slightly raised my hand and weakly admitted, "I am Karen Ann, but I have not done anything wrong."

Then I began to sob. I thought to myself, *"God, here I am, in uniform on my very first trip in the world, and I am not going to get to work? Can this be real?"* Then the airport manager took me aside, while the police officer took the phone from me and picked up the conversation from that point.

The airport manager, whom I had never met before in my life, asked me, "Okay, Honey, will you please tell me what is going on here? Just give me the facts."

In tears, I explained everything to him that I had already told the hotel manager.

I could barely stand, as my knees were so weak from the trauma; I was sobbing as I begged him to help me. "I am on my first actual day of duty – beginning my very first trip. I can't believe what is happening around me. Help me, please, I have not done anything wrong and I do not want to go to jail!"

Thank goodness, the manager patiently listened to me and heard my story, and he somehow knew I was totally innocent. He gave me a hug to calm me down, then he walked over to the police officer and explained to him what was going on, and he retrieved my cell phone from the officer. He handed it back to me, gave me another hug, asking, "Sweetie, are you alright?" I asked him, "Sir, do I get to work my first trip? Do I get to go to work today?"

He laughed and said, "Of course you do, sweetie. I'm sorry for the mix-up. You go and enjoy your first trip." Then he turned and added, "But in the future, be careful what you throw into the garbage cans in those hotel rooms!" He left chuckling.

That day, I learned a lesson I never want to learn again! My second day at work had begun with a nightmare from hell! And little did I know what was ahead of me in this new career - this new journey in my little life!

First Trip

After all the confusion and the threat of jail before I even began my first working trip, I do not recall anything about my first three-day trip. I met and flew with two new flight attendants for the next three days, but I have no idea of where my first layover was for that trip. I flew with the two new attendants, had a good trip, and returned to Chicago where we each went our separate ways, and I found my flight back to Raleigh-Durham International Airport (RDU).

That is when something else kicked in. I began to get a clearer understanding of the term "commute." At home, we considered a commute as a drive over an hour from your home to your office. In my North Carolina hometown, it would require a drive from Burlington, to RTP (Research Triangle Park), or possibly Greensboro.

I found myself driving to RDU, then obtaining my boarding pass for my flight from RDU to Chicago Midway International Airport (MDW), which was an hour and half flight. Then, upon completion of every trip and returning to RDU, I caught my shuttle bus from the airport to the employee parking lot.

It was there that I discovered something of utmost importance. Once I grabbed my luggage and got off the shuttle, I became very embarrassed; I had no earthly idea where I had parked my car four days ago! Although I had a nice (paid for) Honda Accord, I did not have the new up-to-date key, so I could simply punch a button and hear my car beep... ***are you getting the picture?***

I limped around the entire parking lot on my sore broken foot for over an hour frantically searching for my own car, while pulling my luggage behind me. I do recall walking through every employee parking lot. I had *no* idea where my car would be!

In the midst of this search, I made a very important mental note - ***in the future, write down where I left my car!*** The things we learn through experience. Upon locating my car, thank God, I drove home where I learned something else about this new career. While I was home the next three days, I did not have to report to an office, nor was there any paper work to complete, as I was accustomed to. The time I spent with my children and family those next few days were priceless and much appreciated. Not to mention the home cooked meals! My life as I once knew it, was no more. I was embarking on a new way of living – a new lifestyle.

Upon returning to my next trip in Chicago, I was to learn from talking with my crew-member that if I commuted to Baltimore, it would cut my commute time by a half hour flight. But before making the transition, I had to report to my Chicago-based supervisor to make the request.

Before leaving Chicago one day, my girlfriend Kathy, whom I shared my "crash pad"* (See *Tid Bits* after last chapter.) with, asked me if I wanted to catch the train and go shopping in downtown Chicago. I warned her I was on "call duty," but she promised me, "Ann, we can go, and if scheduling calls you, we will just turn around and come straight back." Before I knew it, I was on a train headed for our adventure in downtown Chicago. It was only a 15-20 minute ride, as I took in all the sites along the way. I quickly became the eyes for my mother, calling her and giving her detailed information of all I was seeing!

But guess what occurred? Kathy and I got off the train, walked down the street of Chicago, set foot in Macy's for no more than ten minutes, and my phone rang. It was scheduling! You must understand, when you are on Call Duty, you had better have your cell phone *on* your person, and **On**. *The last thing you want, especially when you are new to the job, is a "Not able to contact" or "No Show."*

I answered my phone immediately. The lady on the other end asked, "Is this Karen? ID46589?" I responded, "Yes ma'am.» She said, "Write this down; we have a trip for you, and you must report to duty within two hours." I wrote down the information, very nervously, very anxiously, and told her, "Yes ma'am." As I hung up the phone, I told Kathy, "Hey! Scheduling just called me! We have to leave now!" Kathy knew the drill, so we did not get to shop for a minute, grabbed the next train back to our crash pad, where I hurriedly packed, and dressed for my report to the airport for duty, and my trip.

THE PILOT'S PAD

Chicago was my home base. It snowed and snowed, and it played havoc on my healing foot. After three months on the job, I was transferred to Baltimore.

I vividly recall my first flight to Baltimore-Washington International (BWI) from RDU. I sat with a very nice first officer, who was especially accommodating to me as a new flight attendant at the BWI base. Her name was Ashley.

As we chatted during the flight, I shared with her that I would begin my next trip in the early morning the next day.

"Where are you going to spend the night once we arrive in BWI?" she asked.

"Well, honestly, I haven't given it any thought," I replied.

"Have you ever been to Baltimore?" she asked.

"No, this is my first time, and I am excited about it!" I believe she picked up on my naivety.

"Baltimore is a large city, and you should not be alone." Then Ashley took me "under her wings" and insisted I ride with her to a crash pad where pilots stayed. It was very late and very dark when we arrived in Baltimore.

"Will male pilots be sleeping there in the same area as the females?" I asked her. I was very uncomfortable about spending a night under the same roof with men, if that were the setup.

She laughed as she explained. "Although there will be men there too, everyone will be asleep for the night as they have very early check-in times in the morning. Anyway, your bed will be in the basement away from everyone else, so there will be nothing to worry about."

So, being alone in the big city, I decided to take her up on her offer, especially since it was already well after midnight. She was right. I did not even see any pilots, because they were already in their private bedrooms sleeping. She showed me to the basement where my twin bed awaited my tired body.

I was thankful for the favor, but I didn't sleep much. I lay there in an unknown place on this new adventure – away from everything familiar to me, thinking about my home, my kids and my parents. I prayed that night all alone in that basement, and gave God thanks for my newfound friend, who had made such an effort to protect me. Once again, the Lord was surely looking after me, and I thanked Him for putting Ashley in my path that day.

As the years went by, Ashley and I actually worked a few trips together, I as flight attendant, and she as first officer. She turned out to be very thoughtful and caring, but also full of humor and practical jokes. I loved being with her. We also commuted many times together over the years. We always sat together, and I would always thank her for the kindness she had shown me on my first night in Baltimore.

On one of our commute trips, I couldn't help but notice the stripes on her uniform. Dear Ashley had been promoted to Captain! I expressed my excitement for her accomplishment, assuring her that she was most deserving of the honor. She knew I meant every word. I was truly blessed to have her as my friend. To this day, I thank God for the many "angels" He placed in my path.

Marilyn

We were on our way to Las Vegas. I was working the middle section of the plane. During the boarding process, I had to stand at the over-wing section, also known as the Emergency Exit Row of the plane. I couldn't help but notice one particularly striking lady who boarded and sat in my designated area.

My eyes must be deceiving me, I thought to myself. This lady looked exactly like Marilyn Monroe! I knew that Marilyn has passed away, but I could not keep my eyes off her because of the stark resemblance. You guessed it. I could not keep my mouth shut. I took the liberty of speaking to her.

"Excuse me, Ma'am, may I ask you something?"

She smiled, "Of course, what is it, honey?" She was beautiful and friendly!

"Has anyone ever told you that you look like Marilyn Monroe? You look just like her... I can hardly believe my eyes."

She laughed out loud and actually gave me a huge hug. She reported proudly, "Honey I certainly hope so! I am on my way to work, where I play the image of Marilyn Monroe, and I get paid big money for this role," she proudly professed.

I had to ask, "How long have you been doing this work?"

"For years! The minute my sponsor saw my resemblance to Marilyn, I was hired for the job. I have taken this flight a lot of years back and forth to work." She beamed with delight!

I had to ask, "Wow! Do you happen to have a picture of yourself in your role, so I can take it home and show it to my mother and kids?" She happily gave me a picture, which of course, I still have to this day.

Marilyn made my day!

Total Silence

I flew a three-day trip with a wonderful guy named Jeff. We had a great crew, and we all worked well together. I had learned early on how much the passengers enjoyed flying with a happy crew, and that particular day, they loved it.

Upon arrival, the plane was on the runway approaching our gate. Jeff was working the back of the plane, and I was working the front with another attendant. Jeff got on the PA system and asked, "Hey Karen. Do you know how to keep over 100 passengers in suspense?"

I responded from the front PA, "No Jeff, how?"

For a long time, there was complete silence. My other crew-member and I looked at each other with a question mark on our faces, like, *when is he going to tell us?* So I got back on the PA one more time, and repeated, "Jeff, how? When are you going to tell us?"

At that precise moment, the entire cabin broke out with laughter. They thought that I and the other flight attendant had supposedly gone along with his game. The answer to the question was ***no answer***...total silence kept them in suspense. The passengers loved it!

As each passenger left the plane, some hugged me while laughing, and others would ask, "Do you and Jeff fly together all the time?" Or something like, "Y'all are a hoot!" Others chuckled, "That was so much fun!"

I had to reply honestly, "No, we just met today and this was our very first trip together." The passengers were amazed! They couldn't believe we had just met and were such a good match. And they so enjoyed the practical joke. I soon realized that jokes and laughter were not only good for the soul, but they also made the flight times seem much shorter.

First Medical Emergency on Board!

I had been working only a few months. We were well in flight and I was working the front of the plane. Suddenly, after having completed delivery of my passengers' drinks and peanuts, I was alerted by a ding, then another ding and then another. I knew something was wrong. Immediately I stopped cleaning the front galley of the plane and turned around the corner wall to see what was happening. I ran down the aisle to the third row of seats on the first officer side of the plane, to find a passenger slumped in the seat -- unconscious.

Everything I had read and been taught in training came to life right before my eyes. This poor passenger was non-responsive. I tapped the passenger on the shoulder, as I had been taught, "Sir, are you okay?" No response. I tried again, "Sir, are you okay? Can you hear me?" Again, no response, no sign of life!

I ran to the front of the plane and immediately notified our captain of our medical emergency so he could call for help. Then, I quickly got on the PA system, requesting all flight attendants to report to the front of the plane for a medical emergency. I also announced that we would appreciate the assistance of any doctors or nurses aboard. This took only seconds.

I promptly returned to our sick passenger in the aisle seat. I repeated the drill, tapping him on his shoulder. I asked him again, "Sir, sir, are you okay?"

Much to my surprise, he opened his eyes, looked straight at me and responded, "Why yes I am, why are you asking, and why wouldn't I be okay?"

I thought to myself, "*Whoa! Is this happening for real? I know what I just witnessed!*" Then I asked him the next question, "Sir, do you know where you are?" I was expecting a simple answer, like "*on a plane.*" But his response floored me!

"Why yes. I would imagine we are about 30,000 feet over Kansas City about now. What seems to be the problem?"

"Sir, you passed out! Do you remember this?" I asked.

"I don't know what you are talking about," he responded.

By then, a doctor on board, along with the other flight attendants from the back of the plane were there to assist, while I went back to the front of the plane to alert our captain of what had just happened.

The Captain responded, "Dang! How in the world could he know that we are 'over Kansas,' if he is in need of paramedics?"

I said, "Sir, I do not know. I know what I just witnessed, and this is remarkable to say the least!"

K.A. Russell

"No worries," the captain responded, "we have already begun our descent to divert the flight so we can get this passenger to the nearest ER. Obviously there is something wrong…maybe they can find out what on earth happened. But how did he possibly know where we were in the air?" Still, we needed medical assistance to find out the real problem as to why he blacked out.

I went back to check on the passenger once again before we landed. That strange experience was a good lesson as to some of the medical emergencies I could expect in the future.

That became my first "diverted flight," meaning we had to land at the nearest airport to seek medical attention for this passenger and send him to the nearest emergency room. This event remains vividly in my memory because we were on our way to Las Vegas, having departed from Baltimore (BWI). We had at least a five-hour, non-stop flight, and had to divert to another city before getting back in the air to reach our final Las Vegas destination.

Before the paramedics transported our passenger in the Jetway, I made a point to gather information as to where they were taking him, so I could contact that hospital the next day. I was relieved when I learned they had checked him in, completed tests and released him the following day. I was grateful he was okay. I was equally grateful that I had just experienced my very first medical emergency at 30,000 feet, and everything that we studied so diligently throughout the training had come to life right before my eyes. I knew I would never forget that incident – ever. It became the first of many medical emergencies over a period of years. I understood that having the responsibility of handling an emergency on board my flight was a very scary and important event that I should never take lightly.

48

FRIENDS FROM THE PAST

I had flown into Connecticut, and I received a call from friends from my childhood, Milton and Betty Wilder. Not only was he my pastor when I was a child; I also was their babysitter when I was 15 or 16 years old for their two little girls. It had been many years since I had seen them, and I was delighted.

Their phone call was to let me know that they were on a trip to the Grand Canyon, Hoover Dam and the vicinity and were staying in a hotel in Las Vegas. They wondered if I might be flying to Las Vegas while they were there. I was excited to reply that amazingly, I was working a flight there the next day and was even staying overnight, something I had not done in months!

That turned out to be a most enjoyable overnight. My crew and I arrived at the hotel, and I contacted Milton and Betty. Instead of my usual walk in Vegas for an hour or so and finding food in the hotel restaurant, I accepted their invitation for dinner. They insisted on driving to the hotel to pick me up. They took me to the Olive Garden restaurant for dinner in Las Vegas (of all the places in the US), and we enjoyed a wonderful conversation of past memories over a great meal, in a state on the other side of the United States, thousands of miles from both of our homes!

We had a blast! While we were sitting there, I called my mom to wish her a Happy Mother's Day. "Mom, you'll never guess who I'm having dinner with way out here in Las Vegas." She was so glad to hear from me, as well as from our pastor and his family of years past. It was a memorable evening.

I learned soon as a flight attendant, to be a little hesitant to make plans such as this, because I never knew when I might be rerouted, due to weather conditions, aircraft maintenance, etc. So to make plans, and actually be able to make the date was indeed a huge deal! We enjoyed our time together in Las Vegas, and they drove me back to my hotel for the night, so I could prepare for my work the next morning. To this day, we still talk about our memorable event in Vegas.

I learned quickly that Las Vegas soon would become one of my favorite overnights, just because I enjoyed seeing all the bright lights. Of all my overnights there, I never gambled once. I just didn't know what kind of luck I would have at such a thing, as I certainly did not know anything about gambling. The bright lights were quite enough for this country girl.

Interview Team

Sometime during my second year at the Airline, there was a request for volunteer candidates for the Interview Team. One had to meet very strict criteria in order to volunteer for this, as it involved interviewing new applicants for the much-coveted position of flight attendant.

I was thrilled to receive acceptance on this team, and I served with great pride and joy.

I found it to be very interesting and challenging. After a few days of this duty, I found it was a huge responsibility as well as a privilege. I was not only interviewing people from all walks of life who wanted to become flight attendants, my much-loved career; I was also screening people to represent the Airline. I understood exactly how they felt while being interviewed, so I was careful to be professional but also kind and understanding.

The job was fun and rewarding, but it also carried the responsibility of having a clear discernment of those who possessed certain qualities. These people potentially would represent the best airline in the world, and they had to be able to demonstrate their ability to treat our passengers with as much loving care as they would their own mother or child. This was Big.

I discovered very soon just how particular I was with my choices. I gained the reputation of being "too picky." I would select maybe one out of every 30 applicants, while other interviewers were selecting five out of every dozen applicants. But I so wanted to select only the perfect candidates.

Remarkably, not long after my year ended on this assignment, I had to report to my supervisor one day at the Baltimore office to ask a question. To my amazement, my supervisor was one of my chosen applicants! He had flown a short time and had requested to become a supervisor. Can you imagine my delight and joy to discover my "pickiness" had paid off; one of my applicants had become my supervisor! He was quite young at his hiring, and had become a fine employee. We became good friends as the years passed. We also shared a good chuckle about the shift of our responsibilities.

Years later, my son in law, Matt, was flying monthly to MDW Chicago. On one of his trips, he was standing in line at the MDW airport, and he struck up a conversation with the flight attendant behind him. You must understand, Matt is very quiet, a man much to himself, so for him to speak was a huge deal.

"How long have you been flying?" he asked.

"Going on nine years," the flight attendant responded.

Matt then added, "My mother-in-law flew also."

"Really? How long did she fly?" he asked Matt.

"About ten or eleven years," Matt answered.

"Do you know where she was based or what year she was hired?"

Matt said, "She was based in Chicago first and then Baltimore, and I believe she was hired in 2001. She also served on the Interview Team."

"By chance, was she a little blonde named Karen Russell?"

Matt was pleasantly shocked and responded, "Yes…that's my mother-in-law! How did you know that?"

Adam responded, "Man! She interviewed me and helped me get my job! Please be sure to tell her hello for me!"

Matt walked away from the line to catch his flight, and sent me a text message:

"Hey there…do you remember Adam? He just spoke to me in line at MDW and said to tell you hello! He said you interviewed him and helped him get his job!"

Matt's news brought tears of joy to my eyes. To think that one of my many applicants, my supervisor, now back as a flight attendant, actually remembered me! It made my day!

Beautiful Sights and a Movie Star

My first trip to California proved to be another unforgettable event. I was working a p.m. trip, which means my crew and I checked into work after lunch in the afternoon and worked through several stops along the way to end our day, and then a layover in Orange County, California. Although it was 11:00 p.m. West coast time, my body remained on East coast time, which was 2:00 a.m. I was anxious to see the sights that awaited me the following morning, after the long haul, so I went to bed immediately upon arrival at the beautiful hotel.

The next morning I arose early, probably not getting sufficient sleep because of my excitement. After showering, I found I was too anxious to have breakfast, so I left the hotel lobby to take an adventure walk.

One cannot imagine my astonishment when those front doors opened and I set foot outside. My eyes focused on a sight that would remain with me the rest of my life. I stood in awe as I saw in a distant view, snow-covered mountains, while in a nearer view the beautiful palm trees and artfully landscaped flowers in full bloom right before me. I was awestruck to put it mildly. I couldn't believe the beauty of this world that lay before my eyes to behold. I immediately called my mother and daughter to describe the stunning sight. Those snow covered mountains in the background in the same view with palm trees and blooming flowers were placed perfectly in the landscaping, and it simply took my breath away.

On one trip, we went through Burbank, California. Although I was seated on the front jump seat, I was responsible for servicing the passengers in the middle section of the plane. I couldn't help but notice a man sitting in the front row of seats on the captain's side of the plane. He looked very familiar to me. Being who I am, sometimes my curiosity gets the best of me. Having been raised in the country, I was engrossed with this new career and the sites along the way. I was also intrigued with the people I met along the way.

After completion of servicing the passengers and taking care of the trash, I commented to my fellow crew-members, "Hey, have you seen that man in the front seat, on the aisle of the captain's side? Man, he looks like someone I have seen on TV." They decided to walk up the aisle to the front of the plane to check out this passenger. (Yes, that's the way we worked - together, as a crew; we were always along for the ride while working our way to our next overnight, wherever it took us.)

My crew-member returned to the back of the plane, only to inform me, "You sure do have a good eye for detail, girl. That happens to be Danny Glover, the actor!"

Wow!! I was so excited I could hardly stand it. So, I immediately grabbed another trash bag, although I had just finished picking up the trash. My crew-members asked me, "Where are you going? Why are you taking up trash again?"

I said, "I can't let this opportunity slip by me! I have just **got** to speak to Mr. Glover!"

They said, "Are you crazy? What if he is unfriendly or doesn't want to be disturbed?"

I replied, "Well, the way I see it, all I can do is try." And up the aisle I went.

I got all the way to the front, stood right beside Mr. Glover, and wouldn't you know it? All I could do was grin, let's say, "like a mule eating briars."

Mr. Glover looked up at me, gave me a huge grin, and asked, "Honey, what are you looking at?"

"**You**!" I continued, "Aren't you Danny Glover?"

He grinned even bigger and responded, "Yes, and I can tell a cute little thing like you is trouble!"

"Man, Mr. Glover, you have made my day! It is a pleasure to have you on my flight. Do you travel with us often?"

"Only when I have to. I do have a home, you know, like you." Then he asked, "Honey, where are you from?"

I proudly announced, "Sir, I'm from North Carolina!"

Laughing out loud, he added, "I would have never guessed it, with that cute southern accent!"

I told him I wasn't the one with the accent, he was. He laughed even harder, adding, "See! I told you that I knew you were trouble!"

"Mr. Glover, may I please have your autograph?" I asked.

"Sure. You give me something to write on and a pen," he replied.

The quickest thing I could think of for paper was, of course, a napkin, which I handed to him, along with my pen I took drink orders with. Once he signed the napkin, his next comment made me laugh out loud. He handed it to me with a huge grin, "Now be sure not to wipe your nose with it!"

I said, "Are you kidding? I will save this napkin for the rest of my life!"

Then, during our final descent, while I was seated on my jump seat again, I couldn't help it. I had to converse with this actor one more time. I leaned around the corner, and he glanced at me again with that huge smile, and asked, "What are you looking at cutie?"

I laughed and responded, "*You*!" Then I said, "May I ask you something I have always wondered about movie stars?"

He replied, "Sure, ask away!"

"How do you remember all those lines you have to memorize?" His answer told me exactly what a kind and humble man he truly is. "Honey, sometimes I wonder that same thing."

I continued, "Thank you for the conversation, my signed napkin, and may I go a step further?"

He laughed, "See there! I told you I knew you were trouble!"

"Could I and my crew member have a picture taken with you?"

"Sure, he said, it'll be my pleasure."

So once we landed, my other crew-member, who couldn't believe my boldness, stood out in the Jetway, and we had our picture taken with Danny Glover. It was an exciting moment, which I treasure to this day. I still have the napkin and the picture, and always take notice of him in movies with this fun memory in the back of my mind.

THE ZIPPER

If you have ever flown on a commercial airline, you have definitely heard an announcement similar to the following: "Ladies and Gentlemen, as we make our final descent into San Francisco, please raise your seat-back into its upright position; please make sure your seat belts are securely fastened, tray tables upright and locked in position; and all items secured under the seat on the floor in front of you. The flight attendants will come through the cabin one last time to retrieve any remaining trash, and it is time to turn off all portable electronic devices and return them to storage.

This announcement is of crucial importance. It means the plane is now at less than ten thousand feet as it prepares for landing and is in final descent. Passengers may not realize that this is the most crucial and dangerous part of the flight. Anything can happen during descent and it is so important to prepare for landing safely.

Flight attendants have the extra advantage of looking out the window of the door next to their seat to see how close the plane is to the ground. The closer to ground, the more dangerous. Passengers absolutely *must* be in their seats during this critical part of the landing!

K.A. Russell

On one particularly memorable flight, as I was looking out the small window of the door next to where I sat on my jump seat in the rear of the plane, I could see buildings and lights. I knew we were only two to three thousand feet above the runway, close to landing.

Suddenly, I turned around to find a man making his way down the aisle to the back of the plane, heading straight for the back lavatory. I wasted no time with my instructions to this man with the command (as taught in training): "Sir! Quickly! You must return to your seat! We are about to land the plane!"

But instead of the man immediately turning around, he decided to argue with me!

"Lady, I must go now!"

"But sir, we are about to land and this is the most dangerous part of the flight!"

But he paid no attention to my words at all; he continued with the same words, "Lady, *now*! Must go *now*!"

I continued with my adamant requests, for what seemed like forever, "Please return to your seat *now*." Suddenly, the man did the unthinkable, especially to the eyes of this little country girl– he proceeded to unzip his pants right in front of me! I quickly covered my eyes (I did *not* want to see this!) and with my eyes covered, I shouted at the man, "Just *go*! Just *go*! Go *fast*! We are about to land the aircraft!"

He wasted no more time arguing with me, ran into the lavatory, and to my amazement, he was in there about one minute! Then, as he ran out of the lavatory and up the aisle, he hollered very gratefully at me, "Thank you ma'am, thank you ma'am!"

Within only four to five minutes, we were indeed on the awaited runway. The plane landed, and thank goodness, the man was safely in his seat. I was still in shock at what had transpired, but very thankful the man was not in the lavatory when we landed!

Did I tell my crew-members of my excitement once the plane was empty? Why, of course I did! They got a charge out of the excitement, but I didn't find a thing funny about it.

UNUSUALLY CALM WIFE

Into about my fourth year as a flight attendant, another of those unforgettable medical emergencies occurred. The interesting thing about those emergencies is that you never forget where the sick passenger is seated on the plane, even in the midst of over 100 passengers.

My crewmembers and I were working in the rear of the plane, when we heard the PA announcement from our crewmember in the front of the plane. We were to report to the over-wing Emergency Exit Row for a medical emergency. We stopped what we were doing and immediately made our way to the scene of the emergency.

The man was seated in the aisle seat on the first officer side of the plane. His wife was seated next to him in the middle seat. We asked him if he was in pain. He shook his head, indicating he was not. We were beginning to suspect he was suffering a heart attack; he was conscious; his skin was ashy in color; and the poor man was sweating profusely.

But the wife interjected, "Don't be alarmed; he is diabetic and needs his insulin." We had already paged for medical assistance of a doctor, nurse or paramedic!

We were on a long flight headed to Las Vegas. (Are you noticing my most crucial medical emergencies occurred on the way to Las Vegas?)

The crew and I were almost convinced we were witnessing a heart attack, and we were still waiting for a doctor to come to our assistance. We anxiously began opening all of the overhead bins looking for his insulin.

"Okay Ma'am! Which overhead bin is your luggage in?"

"Oh, it's not in our carry-on luggage." She replied, seemingly unalarmed.

This poor man was turning darker by the minute, and the sweat was the size of bullets. Finally, we saw a doctor making his way down the aisle to assist us. He asked the wife, "Ma'am, exactly where is the luggage that has his medications?"

Her answer stumped all of us. "It's under us."

"Under your seats?" we frantically asked.

"No," she replied calmly.

"Then where under you?"

"It's under us - in the belly of the plane," she answered in a very unalarmed tone.

We couldn't believe what we were hearing! In the meantime, during all of this confusion, thank goodness, our head flight attendant had notified our captain that we needed to make a diversion to get this passenger off the plane ASAP and to the nearest emergency room.

The most interesting thing about this entire scenario was how very calm his wife was. At first, we wanted to console her, when we realized that she was calmer than we were.

During life threatening emergencies such as this one, you can only imagine how keeping a passenger conscious seems like forever, in order to avoid performing CPR or other critical life-saving techniques.

Finally, we were able to divert the flight, and while we were landing, the paramedics came barreling down the isle of the plane pushing a gurney to put our passenger on. That is when we heard the main paramedic speak in a firm tone to the other medicals, "We have a cardiac arrest on our hands!"

Boy, were we grateful to get that plane out of the air and on the ground, and get our passenger the medical help he needed! During this time, the wife was calmly gathering their belongings. Bet you can't guess what her question to us was? I don't think it's possible, because it blew our minds:

"What time is the next flight to Las Vegas…and what gates?"

That floored us! We were so thankful this poor man made it safely off the flight. We knew the medical professionals would take care of him, as the doctor on board had finally helped him to a stable condition.

As the remaining passengers deplaned, we were a little rattled, but we smiled and said a few kind words to each person as they passed by. We were astonished at his wife's behavior – yes, the entire crew talked about that flight for the duration of our three days together.

Cupid

Into my fifth year of flying out of BWI, where I remained throughout my career, I had the pleasure of working with a wonderful young lady named, Joy a few times. It was by accident that we had several trips together, but they were always memorable.

On one particular trip, we were both working in the back of the plane together. We were on a long flight. It did not take long to discover that any flight less than one hour was considered a "Hop," and anything over three hours was a "Long flight." I can assure you, getting those drinks and peanuts delivered during the short hop flights proved to be a challenge every time, but we always managed to get it done.

On one of our longer flights, my crewmember was telling me about a specific passenger that we had on our flight. "We have a passenger on board who is a pilot with us. He is so dang nice, and handsome; I hear he is an excellent pilot, and I would just love to go out with him sometime!" she whispered to me.

I responded, "Well, does he have your number?"

"No. I have never had the nerve to give it to him." She confessed.

We had finished our drink orders, delivered all snacks, and taken up trash. As we were cleaning up the back galley, I suddenly had another one of those "light bulb" moments.

"If you will point him out to me," I replied to her, "how about when I approach him as I take up trash again, I ask him to come to the back to meet my crewmember who would like to get to know him?"

"Would you do that for me?" She asked with excitement.

"Of course! I will be happy to play 'Cupid!'"

So she pointed out the handsome guy to me; he was seated in an aisle seat, so I figured that made access to him much easier. Shortly, I took up trash again. When I came to the guy she had pointed out, I gently kneeled down on the floor right in front of him. He gave me a puzzled look, somewhat like, *What are you doing?* I then proceeded with my intended role.

"Hello sir, how are you this evening?"

"Great, how are you?" He gave me a big beautiful smile.

I thought to myself, *Well, at least he is responding to me and not brushing off my friendliness.* I continued, "You know what? I am flying with a young lady who has heard nice things about you."

He responded, "Really? That is interesting."

I continued, "Yes sir, she says you have a reputation of being quite an excellent pilot with us."

"Really? That's a nice thing to say." He responded.

I thought, *This looks pretty promising – I will continue.* I then added, "Yes sir, if you get a moment, would you mind coming to the back of the plane, of course while the seat belt sign is off, so you can meet her?"

He said, "Yes, that sounds great."

"Wonderful! When you get a moment, we will look for your visit. Hopefully you can exchange conversation and perhaps phone numbers?"

"I will do it! Thank you very much!" He added.

I then proceeded to continue my trash pick-up, and returned to the back galley of the plane. That is when I found my fellow crewmember engaging in conversation with a man. I thought to myself, *Gee, I wonder who* **this** *man is. I have it all set up for the pilot to come back here, and I don't want to mess it up.*

Once she finished her conversation with the other man, she turned to me, and said, "Wow! I finally got to meet him!"

"Meet Who? Who was ***that*** man?"

"The pilot I told you about!" She was so excited.

I felt like I was going to faint. She looked at me, stopped right in the middle of her conversation with me and asked, "What is wrong? Are you okay?"

"Do you mean to tell me the man who just left is the pilot you wanted to meet and exchange numbers with? That's **the man**?"

She excitedly announced, "Yes! He happened to come back here while you were taking up trash. Why are you asking?"

I then blurted, "If **he** is the pilot you wanted to meet, **who** in Heaven's name is the man I just spoke to about **you**?"

At my words, we both burst out with tummy-hurting laughter, and tears began streaming down our cheeks.

"Who did you think I meant?" She asked, still cracking up. I then proceeded to point down the aisle at the man I had kneeled down before and asked him to come to the back.

"You went to the wrong man! Oh my Goodness, this is the funniest thing I have ever witnessed! This is absolutely hilarious!" she continued as she was still laughing.

I replied, "It may be hilarious to you, but what can I do to clear the egg off my face?" I had to laugh at myself because of the embarrassing situation I had volunteered myself into.

"What do I do now? He is going to come back here shortly, and I can't let him do that; what on earth can I do?"

She said, "I don't know! But I thank you for going the extra mile to help me. But what **are** you going to do?"

I concluded, "There is only **one** thing I **can** do. I will have to humbly approach him one more time, and apologize for making a big mistake."

"Oh my goodness, when are you going to do that?" she asked.

I said, "I have to do it quickly so he doesn't actually come back here. I am going to approach him right now and take care of the 'mistaken identity' problem." So, with no further delay, I took a trash bag down that aisle, and in front of the same strange man, once again, I crumbled to my knees. He put down his book as if waiting to see what this little girl was going to say or do next.

I said, "Sir, excuse me. But I have made a terrible mistake."

"Really? How's that?"

I confessed, "Sir, while I was talking with you, the **real** man went to the back of the plane and met my crewmember. She has already met the man she thought she pointed out to me. I am so, so sorry. I made a mistake. Would you please forgive me?"

He gave me a big smile, "Don't be sorry. I rather enjoyed the compliment and your special attention."

I continued with my apology, "But when I told you she heard you were an excellent pilot..., you are not a pilot at all, are you?"

He then grinned even bigger, "No honey, I am not a pilot."

I then **had** to ask him. "Sir if you are not a pilot, why did you go along with my request? Why sir?"

He quickly and honestly responded with a tremendous smile, "Honey, I decided I would be ***anything you wanted me to be***! It was just too good to pass up!"

My face turned crimson – I felt it. He smiled beautifully again.

"Honey, I will gladly be anything you want me to be, anytime."

I said, "Man, I sure am sorry, thank you for being so kind."

He added, as I managed to get myself up off my knees, "Honey, my offer still goes. I really enjoyed your special attention, and I sure do hope to have you on my flight again! You just made my day!"

I returned to the back galley to find my crewmember. She was eager to know his reaction. When I told her what he had to say, she said, "Wow, Girl! You should go after that man! What a riot! I will remember this story for rest of my life!"

I responded, "You think ***you*** will? What do you think I will do? It will follow me to my grave!" We shared a wonderful laugh, and she did indeed get to meet her pilot and begin a friendship. Wow!

I'm not kidding: ***anything*** can happen at 30,000 feet in the air!

WHERE'S THE MAP?

On another unforgettable flight, just prior to push-back (that's when the plane backs up to head to the runway), my fellow crewmember and I had just completed the safety demo and all eyes were on us because we were facing the passengers. We had taken our places on the front jump seats and were buckling in, when we heard the captain speaking on the PA system.

"Hey dude, where's the map? Do you see it? I can't find the darn thing! Where are we going? Where is the dang map, man?"

My crewmember and I first glanced at each other, then we looked at the worried expressions on the passengers' faces. They looked at us and then at each other. We smiled as we realized we had to remain calm for the passengers' sake.

My co-worker and I didn't quite know what to make of it, because we knew the plane could fly on auto-pilot. So why in the world was he asking about a map on the PA? We sat there motionless and quiet, trying to remain calm, and in our minds, we both were thinking, *Why does he need a paper map anyway?*

It seemed like an eternity and finally, the captain returned to the PA system once again.

"Ladies and gentlemen, we have found the map. Now we know where we are going!"

At that point, my crewmember and I broke out in laughter, as did all the passengers. It was a hilarious moment. The captain had played a joke on everyone, including the flight attendants.

Anytime afterwards when I flew with that captain, I knew what was coming, and I loved it. I knew we were going to have a ball, as it always changed the atmosphere of the otherwise silence during those minutes of push-back.

Flying was always fun for me, but it was always special with that particular captain.

Unhappy Camper

It had been a normal week; flights had been smooth and weather had been beautiful. I believe it was in late 2005, and I was working a six-hour nonstop flight from Baltimore to Los Angeles International Airport (LAX). I could not help but notice a little three-year-old girl as she boarded with her parents. She looked very unhappy, but I decided to ignore it. What a mistake!

After everyone boarded, I took note of where the little girl was seated. She was in her booster seat next to the window on the second row, first officer side of plane, next to her sleeping parents. She still appeared to be very unhappy.

Shortly after takeoff, the little girl began screaming at the top of her lungs, and kicking the back of the seats in front of her. As she screamed, her parents continued to sleep, ignoring her cries. The passengers surrounding the noise began ringing their call buttons, begging me to see what I could do to stop the "terror." It alarmed me not only as a crewmember, but also as a mother, and I could only imagine the thoughts of the passengers possibly having to listen to her screams and put up with the kicking for six straight hours! I received several calls from the passengers seated on the front row, who began asking me to kindly wake her parents and speak to them about their child's behavior.

In an attempt to soothe the bothered passengers around the child, I kindly and ever so gently woke the father, who was seated in the aisle seat. (I had begun to wonder how the parents could sleep through that loud screaming.) I explained to him how she was disturbing the surrounding passengers, and that we had a very long flight ahead of us. I asked him to please calm his daughter. I could immediately tell my request greatly annoyed the father, but he agreed to comply.

Upon completing my drink service, I noticed that the little girl was holding her little hands over her ears as she cried. Again, the mother inside me was overflowing with compassion and sympathy for the child. By this time, the mother was awake.

"Do you think her ears could be bothering her?" I spoke softly to her mother.

"Yes, is there anything you can do to help her?" she responded.

"Yes ma'am, I will try."

I returned to my galley to prepare a harmless and soothing "remedy" that I had been taught via demonstration by a senior flight attendant on one of my previous trips. I prepared the remedy, returned to the parents and directed the mother on the proper use. The parents gratefully thanked me and I returned to my galley.

I was in my workstation hardly a minute, when I heard even more commotion. I returned to the scene, only to discover the mother had not followed my careful instructions, and to make matters worse, the father then began yelling at me. He accused me of being careless and demanded to know my name and ID number. I was shocked! (This kind of attention, I didn't need!)

All the surrounding passengers called me to their seats, offering their names and contact information to use as witnesses. They all noted how tolerant and kind I had been with the situation, and they offered gladly to defend me and my position if it became necessary. After giving it a bit of thought, I also asked the father for his name and contact information. He was furious!

Six hours later, everyone was exhausted from the long flight to LAX, and we finally landed safely. Of course, my flight crewmembers were supportive of me in the entire unpleasant situation I had been forced to endure, noting that I had handled it delicately.

Within just days of completing the trip and returning home, my supervisor summoned me to my home base to explain the situation. Apparently, the father of that little girl appeared to want my blood *and* my job.

Fortunately, the airline knew the circumstances in which I had been placed. As it turned out, the father was the guilty one, for he had intimidated a crewmember (me) while on board a flight and interfered with her duties with his misconduct. I was safe, still with job in hand, and all was well. But I discovered that this situation would follow me through the duration of my flying career.

By the way, soon after the conflict with her father, the Almighty bestowed a special blessing. The little girl fell asleep, only to wake up as we landed. Yes! As they were getting off the plane, the little girl smiled at me over the shoulder of her father. I will never forget the angelic look on her face, as I smiled back and waved her goodbye.

DOWNTOWN

My first trip to Seattle, Washington proved to be a lasting memory. My crew and I arrived early in the morning at the hotel, so I decided to catch a bus to tour the city. I quickly put my things in my room and rushed down the elevator to meet the bus. In my haste, I ran smack into one of the pilots that I had flown with the night before.

"Karen, where are you heading?" he asked.

"Downtown Seattle! I can't wait!" I responded.

"Sweetie, have you ever been downtown Seattle before?"

"No sir! This is my first time, and I am so excited!" I proudly responded. He had caught me off guard.

"Karen, I was on my way to the gym for a quick workout, but you stay right here in the lobby. Don't you go anywhere! Promise me, you will not get on that bus without me! Okay? You do not need to go alone in that huge city!"

"Okay," I promised reluctantly. I had to wait a bit longer than I wanted to, but I kept my promise, and waited on the pilot. It was perhaps a very slow ten minutes that passed by, and when he finally returned, he had dressed to go downtown instead of the gym. We got on the bus and rode and rode.

I finally asked him, "Just exactly how far away *is* downtown anyway?"

He laughed and said, "This is why I insisted you not go alone! It's a long ride, and one could easily get lost not knowing the area."

I was amazed. I couldn't take my eyes off the beautiful scenery along the way. It was breathtaking. I clearly recall the beautiful cedar trees. They were blue-green instead of the ordinary green back home. Everything was a "first" in my eyes, and my new friend knew it by my "oohs" and "wows," as we rode the long road to downtown Seattle.

As we neared our destination, I witnessed the most amazing thing. That bus suddenly became like a trolley car; bars came down out of nowhere and connected to the top of the bus, continuing to take us on our long journey. My eyes were in pure amazement, as that of a child on Christmas morning. My pilot friend just watched me and smiled contentedly.

Amazing! He and I walked and toured downtown Seattle all that afternoon! He took me to the seashore open market, where they were selling "just caught" fresh seafood, beautiful fresh picked arrangements of flowers; different wines, and so much stuff I cannot recall it all. I was in awe. And my friend knew it. He seemed to be amused at my facial expressions and my verbal expressions of excitement!

We toured the shops, until it neared dinnertime, then he treated me to a wonderful steak dinner at a very nice, luxurious restaurant. When the sun began to go down, he said it was time to head back to the hotel. That was when shock and reality set in. He guided us to a group of trolley buses and found the right one to get us back to the hotel. I guess he knew this farm girl would never have found those trolleys!

Unbelievably, the ride back to the hotel seemed even longer than the ride to town. And I knew then, my pilot friend was my guardian angel for the day! I would have surely been lost without his guidance and taking care of me. I realized while on that bus returning to our hotel, I would have never returned to the right hotel; I would have not only been lost, but also I would not have been able to meet my scheduled trip the next morning! I was in shock as the reality was sinking in, and very thankful for my new pilot friend's wisdom and guidance.

Upon return to our hotel, I stopped by the gift shop before they closed since it was late. I thanked my new friend for going with me to Seattle, and he went to his room. I thanked God for sending him that morning; it was certainly no accident that I ran "smack" into him. I went to bed that night dreaming and recalling all of the new and amazing sites of the day, and that beautiful part of the world I had seen with my own eyes. ***Wow***!

A SPECIAL PASSENGER

It was about my eighth year of flying, I was working the over-the-wing position, so I was standing in the area during boarding. About halfway through boarding, I couldn't help but notice a certain man that came aboard. He was extra tall, and had to lean over to enter the plane. As he made his way down the aisle, my eyes were glued to him. I thought to myself, *Can it really be him on my flight? Do I actually get to meet this man? In person?* I was so excited!

As he slowly made his way down the aisle, I studied every feature about him, his face, his hair, his height; I couldn't take my eyes off of him. Finally, he made it to my area. I thought to myself, *What do I say? Would hi be okay?* Finally, the President of the airline approached me, and extended his hand to shake mine.

"Hello Karen."

I shook his hand and responded, very calmly (although deep inside, I was very nervous). "I know who you are! Welcome aboard!" Then I had to ask, "Where are you headed?"

He said he was on his way to a meeting. I told him it was indeed a pleasure having him on my flight, and I was so glad to meet him personally!

Then I went to the back of the plane and asked my crewmember who was responsible for that area of the plane, "Would you mind if I serve the president?"

"No, of course not, if you are willing to ask him to come back here after we complete our drink service and chat a moment with us."

"I will gladly do that!" I replied.

After we completed our service and took up trash, I approached the president.

"The flight attendants would love to chat with you...would you mind coming to the back of the plane."

"Sure, I will be happy to do that!" he replied.

Shortly afterward, he came to the back, where all three of us were gathered. We took advantage of this opportunity, asking him assorted questions. Right now, I can only recall one of my questions. I shared with him that during my nearly nine years, there had been a time in the recent past that had I feared losing my wonderful job.

"Why in the world would you think that? I can already see how lucky we are to have you, what would make you question such a thing?" He responded.

I told him about an unpleasant incident that I had on a flight from BWI to Los Angeles that had caused me to have to defend my job. I added that a disgruntled passenger had overnighted him a five-page letter complaining about me.

Then He placed his arm slightly around my shoulder and calmly assured me, "Karen, do not give that incident another thought! We are proud to have you! Don't lose another night's sleep over that letter or that passenger. Relax and enjoy your work here! We are happy you are here, representing us with that huge smile! Keep up the good work!"

I cannot tell you the relief I immediately felt upon His words of assurance. I did as he suggested. I didn't give it another thought after that. I was grateful to have met in person the president of our airline.

The "Complete Strangers"

It was a usual fall day in October of 2010. Among the boarding passengers was a strikingly handsome businessman, accompanied by a slender businessman friend with a large carryon bag. In a very loud voice, he asked where he could park his large bag, which contained "important files" for his court case tomorrow. It was obvious he wanted everyone to know he was an attorney.

The first officer suggested he try the overhead bins. Because the bag would not fit, he proceeded to remove all the legal binders from the bag. Each one was three to four inches in depth, and he placed all of them in two entire overhead bins. Thank goodness, we only had thirty-seven passengers on board, so there happened to be space available. Usually all of our flights were at full capacity, so this was a rare occasion.

While taking my drink orders, the "attorney" ordered a coke, asking if he could have two cups. This was an unusual request, but I was cooperative and did not question it. The businessman did not order anything to drink, but he leaned across the aisle and said, "Bring him a can; I know him and he will want more."

Later, as I made my way down the aisle, the businessman asked me an unusual question.

"What is the name of your crewmember?"

"Which one?" I casually answered.

"The male one."

"Why do you ask," I responded.

"I am going to write a letter to the airline because he is not recycling your cans."

I asked him, "How do you know this?"

"Because I asked him, and he said, '*maybe*'."

I then attempted to explain that we always put the cans in the same bag as the trash, and then we would separate the cans and put them into the recycle bag when we returned to the back of the aircraft. At that point in the conversation, the passenger interrupted me, waving his hand in my face, losing all composure, and began to shout at me.

"This conversation is over, it is finished!" he said in a loud voice.

I replied, "But…," and he interrupted me again, turning his head away from my attention.

"We will not discuss it any further," he insisted, again turning his head away from me.

During this time, I was unaware that my crewmember, Michael, had been observing the situation from the back of the plane. Michael approached the attorney. "Exactly what is over?" he calmly asked.

The attorney then began rambling as if he was not clear about his story as he blurted, "I am an executive of the airlines."

"What department are you with, Sir?" Michael asked politely.

"You only need to know that I am an executive and this incident will be reported," he replied.

The businessman across the aisle gave the attorney a stern look. "Do not give him any further information…you have said enough!"

I then went to the mid cabin to observe the situation from a distance. I thought to myself, *all of this fuss over a can? Really*? At this point, Michael asked both men to accompany him to the rear of the plane where they could discuss the problem. The businessman gave him a stern look.

"No, this is not going to happen; we are finished with this conversation."

Michael's voice became firm and direct. "You guys have disrupted the duties of the crewmembers during this flight and placed everyone in harm's way. I must insist upon your IDs, driver's licenses, and departments you are with. Make no mistake about it, you will be met by the authorities when we land."

They both smirked, "You will get nothing from us."

Michael had no choice but to contact the captain and asked for authorities to meet them on the ground. After that, the two men gave him their IDs. Michael offered his hand in an attempt to smooth over the situation, but they both refused. When they stepped off the plane, the strangest thing occurred.

I stepped out onto the jetway to witness the conversation between the two passengers and the supervisor. Believe it or not, they claimed they didn't even know each other! The supervisor approached the businessman and kindly asked him if there was a problem.

"Why, no…, I don't have a problem at all, and excuse me if you don't mind, I am going home."

Then the attorney stepped onto the jetway. The supervisor approached him, and asked the same question. He bluntly denied knowing the man across the aisle. "First of all, I don't even know that man; he is a stranger, and I personally don't care if you recycle or not; I throw away everything; it's no big deal to me at all…forget it."

What was this all about? I could hardly believe what I heard. I found it very interesting that when on the plane, the businessman plainly let me know he knew the "attorney" well enough to request a can…and he would want the whole can. While the businessman did not have a drink, he requested I give a can to the "complete stranger;" then he was bent out of shape over recycling.

Unbelievable. All of that confusion over a can? There is probably more to this story than meets the eye. It was all in a day's work, but I was glad it was over.

"No, Mama"

A real emergency took place during the same year of 2010. I call this one *real* because most incidents are not emergencies, thank God. While we were organizing our drink service, all three flight attendants were summoned to the back (AFT) of the plane. A woman was hysterically yelling.

"No, not this! No mama! No! Not now!"

Then she performed chest compressions on her own mother. Recognizing that the passengers were becoming alarmed, I pulled her to the side and spoke to her in a soft voice, trying to calm her down for the sake of her mother, as well as the passengers on board. (Of course, if it were my own mother, I would be doing the same thing she was doing, frantically trying to save her mother, so I understood.)

One crewmember arrived to find the woman unresponsive; (to protect the victim, I will not give details.) Another flight attendant contacted the pilots and medical dispatch. The other flight attendant retrieved the portable oxygen bottle (POB) to attach to the patient, while another flight attendant went to retrieve the defibrillator (AED) in case it was needed. We were holding our breath expecting the worse.

Thank God, a short time afterward, the patient regained consciousness and became fully alert. She looked at us and stated she was *okay*. We were so relieved!

The daughter informed us that her mother was a breast cancer survivor of seventeen years, and she assured us that nothing such as this had ever occurred. The flight attendants kept the pilots informed, while another flight attendant spoke with radio dispatch. The commuting flight attendant who had pitched in to help for one of our crew, who was sick, was such a tremendous help throughout the emergency. She calmly served the passengers and made our jobs much easier. Instead of having to turn back or land prematurely, we were able to settle down for a normal scheduled flight and landing.

Surprisingly, the patient walked off the aircraft without any assistance! Law officers and medical staff were waiting for her. The paramedics were on their way to deliver her to the hospital. Later, we learned the sick passenger had fully recovered and was doing well.

In my mind, I hoped I never experienced another life-threatening emergency like that one again.

No Room

In all my years of flying, and well into my tenth year, the unimaginable occurred upon my arrival at RDU airport. As always, I arrived at the airport well ahead of time, usually an hour or two before my flight to commute to BWI for work. I received my "jump seat" ticket for the next flight. I checked with the ticket agent who informed me it was a full flight, but I should be able to get on without any problem, so I didn't worry.

When it came time to board, however, it was a sold-out flight--even the jump seat was taken. I was distressed. In all my years of commuting to BWI, although I had been "bumped" off my commuter flight before, this time was different. There was not another flight to get me to BWI in time for my check-in. I was in shock. The worst part was that I didn't know what to do next!

For the first time during my commute, I had to call scheduling. They knew from the tone of my voice I was at a loss and under great distress. I asked the person on the other end of the phone, "What am I to do? They have sold out the flight, and I will not be able to make it to check-in time. Please tell me what to do!"

"Hold please, I will be back in a moment," the scheduler said. It seemed like forever. Then she finally returned with instructions: "We are pulling you from your trip since you cannot make it for your report time. There is not a later trip we can place you on, nor another flight that will get you here in time for your present check-in time, so you are free to go home; you will not be working this trip or be paid for the trip. But you will have to work another trip within 30-60 days to make up for the loss of this trip. Do you understand?"

I responded to the scheduler, "Yes ma'am, I understand." She told me I was released from my duties and that I had three days off until my next trip.

As I hung up the phone, I was stunned. In my 10 years of commuting, this incident had never occurred. What was I going to do? I was in uniform, ready to go, bags packed. Everything at home was in order with my children and my daddy. *What now?*

I decided to wait, and ponder exactly what should I do before leaving the inside of the gate area. It was then that I remembered my cousin Sandra, who had just lost her husband to a sudden massive stroke just thirty days prior. I had been so busy working, I am embarrassed to admit that I had not taken time to fly to Orlando, Florida and visit my grieving cousin.

Call Sandra. Go see her now, today. While you are already here at the airport, just hop on the very next flight and go spend some time with her, I thought to myself. So I found myself doing exactly that. I called Sandra, and she was pleasantly surprised to hear from me early in the day. I asked her, "Do you have any plans for today? If I flew to MCO (Orlando International Airport), could you pick me up at the airport and could I spend the night with you?"

She responded, "Yes! Come on down here! We will have a nice dinner and catch up. Come on down!" With those words, I jumped on the next flight to MCO.

We enjoyed a wonderful evening talking over dinner together. While I was in MCO, I knew I needed to pick up that other trip to replace the one I had missed. I was fortunate to locate a trip flying out of MCO; I shared this information with Sandra, so she could be prepared to get me back to the airport the next afternoon.

The following morning, while drying my hair, with my head bent over toward the floor, I noticed the floor ever so slightly moved toward the right.... then upon raising my head, I noticed the ceiling slightly moved toward the right as well, the exact same thing the floor did. I thought to myself, *Hmmm. We must be having an earthquake like the one in Japan last week.*

I wandered into the living room where I asked Sandra, "Hey, did you see that? The floor and ceiling just moved." Sandra shot me a funny look, stating very matter of factly, "No," adding "Come here, and let me take your blood pressure." As an RN and very good in her field, I let her take my blood pressure. It was perfectly normal.

She insisted, "You need to eat something, maybe a banana, because something isn't right. You certainly do not need to be getting on a plane today!"

"But I have to. I have a trip on my screen and I must report for it." Once again, a little annoyed by then, she insisted, "Now you be sure to call the doctor when you get home. I'm telling you, you shouldn't be flying with that dizziness."

I promised her upon my return home, that I would get to the doctor, but in my mind, I thought, *Only if the dizziness continues.*

WHO?

I arrived at the Orlando airport, checked in at a computer for my trip, as usual, and waited to meet my crew, as I had not flown out of MCO before. We boarded the plane and worked the flight with no difficulty. We overnighted in Indianapolis (IND). Upon arrival at the hotel for the evening, I went to the gym and worked out a short while before ordering dinner, taking it to my room for the night.

I set my alarm for a 3:00 a.m. wakeup, as I had to be back in the lobby by 5:00 a.m. the next morning. At nine o'clock, I decided it was time for bed.

I had been asleep only a short time; my head was hurting enough to wake me. I glanced at the clock beside my bed. It was 11:00 p.m. I had only been asleep a couple of hours. But as I sat up in my bed to go take a Tylenol for my headache, something unforeseen occurred. The room was spinning out of control. It made the Wizard of Oz look like a joke. I immediately laid my head back down on my pillow to make it stop, only to realize that lying down only made it worse! Then my entire body began to spin with the room! What was *this* all about? My head was pounding from the pain; my body was spinning in a spinning room. I wondered if I were dying.

I grasped for my cell phone, which I had learned to keep by my bed when away from home and family in case of an emergency. I tried again to sit up in my bed, only to realize this was not going away. Then came the sickening feeling we all know too well -- nausea. I thought, *Oh my God. What am I going to do? I can't even sit up straight! How on earth can I possibly make it to the restroom to losing my cookies?* But I had to…I didn't have a choice in the matter.

With the room spinning out of control, my entire body spinning with it, topped off with an overwhelming nausea unknown to mankind, I literally slid like a snake out of my bed, found my way to the floor on my hands and knees, and crawled to the bathroom. Little did I know what lay ahead of me, and thankfully, a little voice reminded me to take my cell phone.

It felt like I was losing everything in my entire body. I prayed. I pleaded… *God, am I going to die here, tonight, away from my children, my daddy, my family? What is happening, God? Help me, Lord! Help me! Are you taking me home with you? Am I coming to see you and mother?* So many thoughts and questions raced through my scrambled mind. I glanced at the cell phone only to discover I had been losing everything in my body for an entire hour. I didn't know what to do!

I knew I needed to call someone, but who? I thought to myself in my sick, dizzy, spinning head. What amazed me most about the whole situation was that during all of the dizziness, I had to think! Thinking was just too much! *Okay. I need help. But* **who?** *And at this hour of the night? It is now midnight.* **Who** *is going to have their phone on?* The biggest question of all remained– **Who?**

Then the spinning picked up in speed even worse as I had to try to think. It went something like this, to the best of my recollection: First, I tried a text message to my flight attendant friend. But there was no response. According to my cell phone, all I was able to write were the words, *"sick need help."*

Then the rationalization began all over again. Trying to think was the hardest thing I had to do. *My daughter has an infant at home, so she shouldn't leave him. My son is a pilot; he has a wife, and he needs to report to duty, so I can't contact him either. And besides, I do not want to scare my children half to death in the middle of the night. They were hundreds of miles away, and they could do nothing but worry.*

Then I remembered Sandra. She saw me last. She knew something was wrong that morning. Call Sandra. I called the last number dialed in my phone – to Sandra, but thinking, *Oh man, what if her phone is off? What if she doesn't answer?* But much to my amazement – she answered! "What's going on?" she asked.

I told her everything that was happening to me. Sandra is truly an RN at heart. She knew immediately what to say to me. She was very straightforward, very simple, and affirmative.

"Ann, you must go to the nearest emergency room as soon as possible! You need to call the hotel front desk."

I asked, "***How?*** I am too sick."

She ordered me, "Crawl to the table beside your bed. Can you do that? Crawl to the phone; dial zero; tell the front desk you need to get to the ER ***ASAP***. You are sick and do not know what is wrong…Ann, can you do this?"

I remember crawling back to the night table beside my bed and the great effort it took to get there, and the even greater effort it took to dial zero. I spoke with the operator, because she kept asking me if I was "sure." I emphatically said, "Yes, help me, please! ***Now!***"

To this day, this whole scene astounds me. I am a Flight Attendant, trained to take care of people, especially in the event of emergencies. And yet, I was…completely and utterly helpless to help myself. Sandra had to instruct me on each small detail. I could not have made that call to get help without Sandra's detailed words of instruction. This was serious business. I didn't know if I was dying or not in that hotel room away from my family.

PARAMEDICS AND PANTIES

Within minutes, I heard the paramedics shouting outside my hotel door. The lady shouted loudly, "Ma'am, ma'am, do you need help?

I was lying on the floor on my tummy, still losing my cookies, with everything spinning all around me.

I weakly responded, "Yes ma'am, help me, please!"

"Please release the chain on your door, so we can enter your room and help you!" she yelled.

I thought to myself, *How can I do that? I can't get off this floor. God! Help me! Please!*

While these thoughts were racing through my mind and weak body, again came the demand from outside my door, "Ma'am, release the chain! Now!"

I found myself crawling on my knees, head down. I made my way to the door, which seemed like miles away. I remember keeping my head tilted down, so I would not dare raise it to look up. I stretched my arm and grabbed hold of the door handle, pulling myself up quickly, and with all my might quickly jerked the chain out of the latch. It took enormous strength to accomplish what seemed like an impossible task. The instant I jerked that chain out of the latch, I fell to the floor not raising my head.

The paramedics entered the privacy of my hotel room with a stretcher. I never saw them; I only heard voices as they went about what they needed to do. I remained on the floor while the paramedics went through my entire luggage, my medications, and everything I owned. I was so sick, there was a slight detail I didn't realize.

"Lord have mercy, sweetie...you don't have any panties on!" She said. "Get me her panties, please...quickly."

I was so sick I really didn't care. "Please help me! The room is spinning out of control and something is terribly wrong!" I pleaded.

"It's going to be alright in a minute sweetie; first I have to get the IV in your arm to stop the nausea."

After they finally put on my panties and pajamas, they raised me to the top of the stretcher, where I had to lie on my side in case I threw up again. As they strolled me out of the room and down the hall, the men were talking among themselves.

"Hey man, have you ever been in this hotel?" The other man replied, "Naw man! This is a nice place. Look! Man, this is nice!"

They rolled me into the elevator, off the elevator, and straight through the lobby of the hotel. That is when the woman yelled to the clerk at the front desk, "Mister! We have a flight attendant. We are taking her to the

ER. Make sure nobody goes into her room. We don't know what is wrong with her, but she's awful sick!" The clerk responded, saying he would keep the room locked.

I heard all this and I still had not laid eyes on any of these people taking me away from my room to the hospital. I still can't believe it happened. Then something strange occurred. I heard a man speak to me in a very soft-spoken voice. He was on the same side of the stretcher that I was facing. He leaned into me and asked, "Honey, are you a flight attendant?" I vaguely remember nodding my head up and down for "*Yes.*" I never saw his face either.

"Honey, I am too. Would you like me to go with you to the hospital so you will not be alone?"

Once again still not seeing a face, I nodded my head up and down for "*Yes,*" but I recall saying, "Only if you want to." I didn't want to bother anyone, especially on the job. I thought he must have been an angel.

I never saw any of the faces behind all the many voices I heard while being pushed on the stretcher or being put into the ambulance. I remember someone asking me which hospital I wanted to go to. I simply answered, "The closest one." The "angel" actually sat by my side in the ambulance and went with me to the hospital ER. He comforted me until I fell into a deep sleep, thank God. I later learned the man that went with me to ER was Randall, when he called Crystal.

I do know this. In hindsight, this angel of a man saved my job. He called scheduling to inform them of my sudden illness and alerted them I was in the ER. If he had not made the phone call, I would have received my only "No Show" or "Unable to Contact." You must understand, I was unable to make that call to my work on my own. I was unable to be fully responsive to anyone or anything. I wasn't even able to contact my own children – this man did! I was utterly helpless, and semiconscious. I only recall his whisper into my ear letting me know he had to leave me because he had to return to the hotel to report for his own trip. God bless this man! He left me in the ER, while I overheard the nurses and doctors saying, "Aw, she is probably just intoxicated because she is a flight attendant." I was unable to defend myself as I went in and out of sleep, but I recall how annoyed it made me to hear the words, because I am not a drinker. I stayed in the ER until they relocated me to a different room.

A Dark Room

I remember slipping in and out of a deep sleep. Every time I even tried to raise my head off the pillow, the room would begin to spin. Then the nausea would return. *Oh, my God. What is happening to me, and where am I?*

The nurses rarely came in to check on me. They informed me they had taken me out of the ER and placed me in a private room. I remember it was dark all the time. *Why?* Then a nurse told me she was taking me in a wheelchair down the hall for a doctor to re-examine me. I told her I didn't feel like going, but she said it was procedure. They had to perform a "maneuver" on me. I thought to myself, *What is a maneuver and what does this mean?*

Then a doctor instructed me to get up out of the wheelchair and lie flat on my back on the bed. I did not have the energy to perform these tasks, nor did I want to move my body. But he insisted. It took everything in me to do as he instructed. I lay down on the flat bed. Then he told me he was going to perform a maneuver. (That word again). I had no idea what he meant by a maneuver but I complied without putting up a fuss.

I still felt awful. I did not know what was wrong with me, going in and out of consciousness.

He took my head in the palms of his hands and he kept turning it all the way to one side and left it in that position for a long time. I just recall him turning my head from side to side in very quick movements without warning me, and it upset me!

I hollered, "Oh my God! Why did you do that? It's sooo bad! Please make the spinning stop!" The spinning was just as it was in my room that night, and I knew what was ahead of me then…more nausea.

I shouted at him, "I do not like you! Why did you make it worse? Why did you do that? You are not a very nice man! And I do not drink."

"Just let her sleep it off," he said, ignoring my comments.

After that "maneuver" which I was quickly coming to loathe, the nurse strolled me back into that dark room.

"That doctor is not a nice or compassionate man and I do not like him." She did not respond, as she put me back in my bed in that dark room.

So I fell back to sleep. As I dozed off, I prayed, "God, where are you? Where am I? Where is my family? What is wrong with me God? Please help me God!" Then I fell into a deep sleep again.

When I woke up, a nurse brought me a hospital phone. She told me I was in a hospital and had been there two days. I said, "What? Two days? Does my family know? What about my children?"

She said the room they put me in would not pick up a signal for a cell phone, so they put a hospital phone in my room in case my family tried to contact me. So I fell asleep again, soon to be startled by the irritating noise of a phone ringing. I struggled in the dark to find the phone.

It was Crystal. "Mama, we are so worried about you! What has happened to you? I am so glad you are alive, thank God!" I told her I was very sick. I told her the doctors said I was intoxicated. That made her so angry. "Mama, you don't even drink! How dare them! Mama, how do I get there? I need directions to get there?"

I told her not to come because she had a new baby at home, an infant. I told her I was sick and the room was spinning, and that I slept most of the time because the room didn't spin when I was sleeping.

She kept saying, "Mama, you do not need to be there alone! One of us needs to get there to help you!"

We talked a little while, and then I was too tired to keep talking and told her I needed to sleep. She knew that was not like me. I always talked and had something to say and plenty of it. *My daughter hasn't heard from me in days, and I want to sleep?*

At some point, a lady from the airline came into my room. Although she introduced herself, I do not remember her name or seeing her. She said she was there to see what she could do to help me. I don't recall if I was kind to her or not, because I was not myself, I did not feel good, so I didn't feel like having visitors.

"Where is your luggage?" I told her I didn't know. She asked me, "Is it still at the hotel?" I told her again I didn't know. Then she asked, "Would you like for me to go to the hotel and bring all of your luggage and personal belongings to you?"

"Yes. That would be very nice." I responded.

Then she said, "You are the first flight attendant I have been contacted to help." She sounded excited about it and left. Then I slept again.

I woke up sometime later to see my luggage in the room against the wall. I fell asleep again, not remembering if I had thanked her or even said goodbye.

A Friend Indeed

My girlfriend, Glenda was asleep in the hotel room when she received a text message from Crystal who had called her after speaking with me on the phone. Glenda went downstairs to the hotel computer to see what was on my schedule for work and it showed that the scheduler had pulled me from my trip in Indianapolis and I was on sick leave. After seeing my schedule, she immediately called Crystal and instructed her to tell the hospital staff not to release me, as I had good insurance, and that I was in no condition to return to my hotel, much less report to work on the plane the following day.

Crystal called the hospital to inform them I needed to stay until someone could get there to take me home. It appeared the hospital was anxious to release me without finding out what was wrong. To this day, it amazes me how the hospital was trying to "run me through and get me out as quickly as possible," before they even tried to get to the bottom of what was making me so sick and unable to communicate.

My big brother, Darrell, and his wife were getting ready for the long road trip to come to my rescue. Brad was also trying to work out his flying schedule to come and help me. As you might guess, I was unaware any of these communications. Finally, on my third day, Glenda was able to catch a flight and come to the hospital. She spent the next four days with me, trying to find out what exactly happened. The first day she arrived (my third day in the hospital), she brushed my teeth, as they had not been brushed since I had been there. She also sat me in a chair in front of the sink in the rest room and washed my hair. When I think about it now, I know the nurses were not taking care of me as a dependent patient.

Upon a visit from the doctor, I recall his words shaking me up a bit. He bluntly said, "You will not be able to continue your career in flying. If you work at all, it will need to be a land job." His harsh words made me depressed and angry. I remember telling the doctor, "Oh yes, I will continue my job! I will! I am going to get better."

Then we asked him, "Doctor, what were the results of the MRI?"

"The tests did not reveal a tumor, so we are going to label it vertigo, since she says she doesn't drink." He also concluded, "There's something else going on that we cannot identify. We just can't put our finger on it."

"What is vertigo?" I asked.

"Dizziness, room spinning, nausea – all of your symptoms," he replied.

I didn't care what the doctors said about my work. I continued to argue with them on that issue. I wanted to return to my much-loved job.

Glenda went to get food the day before we checked out of hospital. I didn't have an appetite, and I was surely afraid if I did eat, I wasn't sure what the consequences would be. She rented a car to drive me home because I couldn't fly due to my sickness.

We finally arrived at my home on April 2. By this time, I still did not have an appetite, but I was happy to be out of the hospital and back home with my children and my family. My girlfriend was kind enough to stay a week with me before going back to work. During the week she stayed with me, she drove me to my regular physician; then she drove me to see an ENT specialist. Much to my disappointment, the doctor's words were the same as the doctor at the hospital in Indianapolis, "You will not be able to continue your job in flying. There seems to be more going on than the eye can detect, so deep behind the wall of the brain that the MRI cannot pick it up." And once again, I refused to listen to his comment, arguing that I would go back to my job. "I will!"

My girlfriend had to leave to return to her own home. It was then that daddy commented, "A friend in need is a friend indeed."

First Year Out of Work

The following weeks, I vaguely recall my daddy and my brothers dropping by my home to check on me. Crystal took me to several different doctors. I do recall my pastor, Reverend Baughn, who would stop by and visit briefly, as he realized I was not myself.

He constantly said, "I am worried about your job."

I always argued with him, "I'm not; I am going back to flying; that's my job and I love my job."

He always commented, "I'm afraid you will never be able to work that job again." Each time I would dismiss his words.

No one understood what was wrong with me, and neither could I. I recall the room spinning every time I would lie down. I discovered the only way I could sleep in my bed at night was to stack three pillows on top of each other. I spent most of my nights lying awake in worry and anxiety.

Then I began to wonder what I *could* do; *if I can't sleep or fly, maybe I can still type. Type about what?* That night I got out of bed and sat at my computer from 2:30 a.m. until 5:30 a.m. the next morning, and I could indeed type. I began to write thoughts about my sweet mother, who had passed away with leukemia five years earlier. I discovered I was still grieving over my loss, and my heart had not healed. So every night that I could not sleep, I would pick up in mother's story where I had left off. Finally, I had a purpose! The amazing thing was that my long-term memory held all those thoughts, but I could not remember recent things in my short-term memory. It was by the Grace of God I was able to write, especially about mother, but I did. Then by 5:30 a.m., worn out from staying up half the night, I would take my anxiety medication and sleep most of the mornings, sometimes until midday, I embarrassingly admit.

All I really remember about the days, weeks, and months that went by was going from specialist to specialist. Crystal knew I shouldn't drive, so she drove me to my appointments. Once I began feeling better, I would only drive to Crystal's home to spend time with my baby grandson, or to see my daddy – both of them live only a short distance away.

During that time, I found it difficult to keep up with my appointments and keep my household bills paid. My memory seemed to come and go. In all honesty, I recall very little of my first year out of flying. I just remember the great mental energy it took for me to remember *anything*, and to *think*.

I found myself on short-term disability for the first six months out of work, so I only received one-half of my usual monthly salary. I was guilty of being angry with God for my sudden inability to work the job I loved so much.

THE BIBLE STUDY

My daughter, Crystal asked me to join her in a weekly Bible study at the church she attended. At first, I flatly refused, explaining, "I am pretty angry with God right now. Besides, how do I know if I will even be able to understand or retain anything because of the mental state I am in?"

"Awe, mom, please go with me this one time. It will be good for you... please.""

I gave in, as it was (and still is) hard to say "no" to my daughter and best friend. Crystal had no idea what the study would be about that day. It was, *Jonah: Navigating a Life Interrupted*. **Yes**! That got my attention. My life had been totally interrupted! I had lost my health, and was unable to perform the job I enjoyed more than anything. Yes! I was living "a life interrupted!"

I sat during the session that first week, and just listened to the teacher and other women's questions and comments in the study. It was the story of Jonah – you know, the man in the Bible who stayed in the belly of a whale for three days. I had heard the story all my life, but it had never affected me the way it did that day.

During the second week of the study, I sat beside Crystal, listening to other women telling what a wonderful God we served, and how He had blessed us beyond measure. I sat there, quietly, as long as I could stand it. Then, Crystal observed me pushing my book away from me on the table, and sliding my chair away from the table. I'm certain, she was thinking, *Uh oh....mama is getting ready to say something...uh oh! This is 'gonna' be good!*

She was right. I stood up. I believe my words went something like this.

"Okay. I am a believer. I have loved and trusted God since childhood. But seriously, as I sit here and listen to all of you saying how wonderful God is, I have to ask, am I the only one in this room who is angry at God right now? I have been a flight attendant for ten years now for a company I love. I am a single, divorced woman. Just recently, after asking God to give me good health so I could continue to work, I got terribly sick on a layover. To this day, not even one physician has determined what is wrong with me. And I cannot fly any more right now; I am frustrated; I am confused; I miss going to work each week. In the blink of an eye, illness stopped me dead in my tracks. So yes! My life has been interrupted! And I am not happy about it at all. One of the hardest things is that I am accustomed to working every week on a job I love. I am no longer in control of my health, my life, or the outcome. I need answers."

Then as I took my seat, a few more women actually admitted they were upset with their lives, and they were seeking answers too. So I wasn't the only one searching for answers from God in the midst of storm. Good!

Through that Bible study, I learned that Jonah had gone in the opposite direction from where God had instructed him to go, but more importantly, that God was a God of second and third chances. I realized that my life had been interrupted as it had never before, but I didn't understand why. I had no choice but to admit my failure and lean on God for the answers.

And as life would have it, the following morning on TV, I tuned in to a well-known godly woman teacher. Do you know what she said? "You know, sometimes people get angry with God. Why would they get angry at the only one Person who can Help them, and the Only One who has the Power to help them?"

I nearly fell off the couch; she had put me in my place. I immediately realized my mistake, and asked God to forgive my ignorance and for being angry at Him. Right then, I wanted God to heal me at that very moment, at that very place. I wanted to get well and get back to my job. It did not happen.

As time passes, I can see and feel myself getting better, and I know in my heart that I will be completely well again soon!

An Old Friend

After the six months of short term disability income ceased, I was then forced into long term disability. This meant my half-salary was increased by only ten percent – not much when a person has a home and car payment. I thank God that He allowed me to keep both of them.

I began cleaning out my closets, with what little energy I could muster and took things to consignment shops to sell just to help get enough funds to make ends meet. Unfortunately, in my dizziness and inability to think straight, I didn't realize until I began to heal, that I had accidentally taken some things that I shouldn't have and later really needed.

On one of my trips to the consignment shop, a lady spoke to me calling me by my name. "Karen. Is that you? I haven't seen you in such a long time!"

Looking at my puzzled face, she said, "Karen? Are you okay? Are you still flying?"

"How do you know my name? No, I haven't flown for several months, but how do you know I fly?"

"Karen, something has happened to you, hasn't it? You remember me? I work for Gary Bailey, your counselor from years ago?"

That's when things began to come together and make some kind of sense. I said. "Yes, Gary… how is he doing?"

Then she added, "Karen, is it okay if I tell Gary I saw and spoke with you?"

"Please do. I would love to hear from him," I responded.

I am convinced that running into Venice that particular day God Himself planned. I believe Gary called me that same day. We set up an appointment for me to come into his office for a counseling session.

Gary knew me well enough to know that something had happened, and the Lord knew I needed someone with wisdom to talk with. For that time in my life, he was a gift from God to me. He helped guide me in making extremely important decisions regarding my insurance bills, my disability, questions to ask doctors; the list was endless. He kept me on track, so to speak. He also tested my cognitive skills, looking for answers.

He counseled me on how to hold on to my flying career, because he knew how much it meant to me. He knew my plan was to fly at least ten more years before retiring. At least that was *my* plan. Now I know how God must get a real kick out of mankind and their big thoughts and plans.

When people are on any type of disability, they must go to the doctor at least once a month or at least in two months. For me, this back and forth to the doctor was draining physically and mentally. After each visit, the doctor had to complete forms and send a copy to my employer so I could hang on to my job. I was determined I was going to get better and return to my job.

The longer I was out of work, the harder it was to meet with friends. I reached a point that I did not desire company except my immediate family. I didn't want to have to answer their questions, because having to think was so strenuous on my emotions.

But the many MRI tests and CAT scans always came out negative, leaving everyone in the medical field stumped. Something was wrong indeed, but what in the world was it? I always thanked God there were no tumors revealed through the many tests, but there were no real answers. It was so frustrating: *if nothing is wrong, why do I feel so bad?*

One day out of the blue, my dearest and best friend from first grade, Sylvia called. She had been a nurse all of her life, and an excellent one. She asked if she could come visit me. In all honesty, I can't recall when she called or when she started visiting me. But I know that she came about once a week. Sylvia remarked that my speech was not normal. Sometimes I could not get a word out of my mouth. Anyone who knows me knows I always have something to say, so it was quite embarrassing for me not to be able to carry on a good conversation. I would be talking to a family member or friend, and I could always tell when things were not coming out correctly, because they would look at me strangely, waiting for me to try to finish a word, much less a sentence.

Sylvia and I met for lunches or dinners as often as I felt up to it. On several occasions as I attempted to pay for my meal in cash, Sylvia noticed I was unable to count the right change. She had to assist me in paying the bill. That told her something was very wrong. But what? After those embarrassing moments, I tried not to use cash anymore, and instead used my debit or credit card to save the embarrassment.

WALKING THROUGH THE FIRE

It was well into my second year that I was unable to fly, and Crystal was still driving me to my doctors' offices at least once a week. At that time, I could not remember how to get to all the locations for the MRIs and CAT scans. At each visit, doctors told me, "Karen, you will not be able to work again." I refused to listen to those words.

"Karen, are you exercising?" one doctor asked.

"No sir," I answered.

"Maybe you should join a gym or something to get some physical exercise," he suggested.

I was on disability -- one half of the regular salary that I was accustomed to, and I knew I could not afford the cost of a gym, so I began to think of ways to exercise at home. Another one of my "light bulbs" came on. *I live in the woods, and there are so many unwanted leaves.* So I decided to get physical exercise in my yard by raking leaves for a few hours a day. I also recall in my prayer time that particular day, I had asked God to give me a "productive day." I was asking Him to show me just how much production my body was able to accomplish.

It was good physical exertion but very exhausting. I discovered I only had the energy to rake maybe an hour or two per day. This told me just how weak my body had become. I didn't have much energy, but I was determined to exercise as the doctor ordered.

So little by little, every day I raked, and raked, and raked. I began on one side of my driveway. I do not recall how long it took, maybe two or three weeks, but after getting them all raked up, I do recall lighting the match to burn the pile of leaves. It was a little scary and extremely hot, but I was getting exercise and getting rid of the unwanted leaves at the same time! I accomplished the task on the one side of my driveway. After completion of the one side, I took a break for a week or maybe two, and then I pursued the other side of the driveway, doing exactly as I did on the previous side.

I raked and raked, and made piles and piles of leaves. Then just like the other side, I decided to get rid of the ugly leaves and struck another match. I recall being a bit surprised at how quickly this pile of leaves caught fire, as on the other side of the driveway it was a challenge just to get the fire started. Then I turned my back to rake more leaves into that pile. My mistake was in turning my back.

It had only been about five minutes...then I turned around to see the unthinkable! The fire burning that pile of leaves was crawling through my woods, under my picket fence into my backyard, **and** crawling into my next-door neighbor's yard!

I could not seem to think what to do; my thoughts were, *Why on earth is this happening? Why aren't these leaves just like the others I burned? What am I going to do?*

I panicked! I was running all over the place chasing that fire that was crawling **out of control** – everywhere! It was behind my storage building; it was taking over my neighbor's yard! I had to **think**! So I put down the rake and exchanged it for a water hose connected to my house. The spray handle was unattached, and I couldn't waste time to get it, so I used my thumb to try to make it shoot farther. I concentrated on the area behind my storage building and my neighbor's yard, which by that time was half burned! I was trying so hard to think about what to do that I had neglected to look at my own yard, because the fire was then crawling under what used to be a very pretty picket fence that was covered in smoke and blazes. Then I realized the fire was heading toward my propane gas tank! Then I started **praying**! *"**God! Help Me!** I don't know what to do!"* By this time, I glanced at my cell phone in my pocket and realized I had been fighting the fire for an hour! I believe that is when I called Crystal and told her what was happening. She said she would be right over!

Then a stranger drove right into my driveway, and I was standing in the middle of the flames and smoke. She got out of her car. I shouted, "**Help**! Help Me! Please!"

She asked me the million-dollar question: "Have you dialed 911?"

"No ma'am." I admitted. *(I had not even thought of it.)*

"Have you called the fire department?" she screamed! *(I had not thought of that either!)*

116

"No ma'am, will you do it for me?" She did it right then!

Within minutes, *three* fire-trucks appeared, while I was still running from left to right, still attempting to keep the fire away from my propane gas tank and hoping it would not go "*kaboom*!" Thank God, the firefighters immediately jumped out of their trucks, and they began running all over my flaming front yard, to the back yard where my gas tank was, and my neighbor's yard, and I was running alongside some of them, all the while asking, "How did this happen?" They looked at me kind of funny like, *Did she really ask me that question*? I explained, while out of breath, that I had burned the leaves on the other side of the driveway with no problem. I asked them to tell me why the leaves got out of control on *this* side of the driveway!"

That is when I learned some valuable information. The fireman explained to me, "Well on this side of the driveway your neighbors have pine trees in their yard. Therefore, under the dry leaves, there are also dry pine needles. And believe me, dry pine needles are worse than gasoline! That's why the fire was "crawling!" I couldn't believe what I had just heard. I must have been a sight; soot, sweat and pine needle smoke covered me, and I was a total wreck!

It took the three fire trucks about an hour to put out the bonfire I had started. I was as nervous as a cat walking around on a hot tin roof! When the fire was finally out, I suddenly realized the extent of the damage it had done, not only to my yard and fence, but also to my neighbor's yard!

"Oh my God! I am gonna get sued over this for sure! And *how* am I going to pay for it?"

Crystal had finally arrived. She was as stunned as I was. She was more concerned over my wellbeing than the damage. But she was in shock at the sight before her eyes. After every hint of smoke was out, Crystal and I went into my house. I cried, "Oh no, now I have to go and face my neighbors and beg for their forgiveness, and more importantly, pray they do not sue me! Crystal, what am I going to do?" I cried.

"Mama, do you want me to go with you?"

I cried, "Yes, please go with me! I need your help and support, and I need my neighbor's ***mercy***!"

So we walked through the burned ground over to my neighbor's house. We didn't even get close to the front porch, when the front door opened and out stepped my neighbor. Why, she was there all along – watching the whole thing! I was in tears at the thought of facing her.

"Honey, are you okay?" She asked.

I wept as I said, "Ma'am I am so very sorry! I still don't know how it got out of control like that! Can you ever forgive me? I am ***so sorry***!"

Her next statement floored both Crystal and me. She said, "Honey, I am just sorry you even called the fire department. I would not have cared if the whole darn yard had burned up!"

I looked at Crystal; she looked at me; we were in shock. I replied, "What did you say?"

"It was such an eyesore anyway, and I have asked my husband to clean it up, but he hasn't been able to. So, I was hoping the whole dang yard would just burn up!" She replied.

Then all three of us broke out laughing. I looked at Crystal and said, "Man! Talk about *mercy*! I just got a heaping spoonful of it!" Crystal laughed until tears streamed down her cheeks.

Happily, we walked back across the ashes and soot to get home so I could take a shower. Before we could get into the house, my daddy, Matt, and my grandson, Will, came by to see what the excitement was all about.

It was then that my wise, 84 year-old daddy spoke, "I have known all along that something besides 'vertigo' was wrong with you, now I have witnessed your lack of ability to process things properly...and the energy level you used to possess is gone. Now I have seen it for myself."

Daddy hit the nail on the head! All that time I was trying to think what to do, I could not even remember about 911 or the fire department! All I thought about was, if I could not put out a fire, I was not capable of being a flight attendant.

After my shower, I found my family members still there, waiting to make sure I was okay, mentally and emotionally. As we sat around talking about the commotion I had caused, I chirped up and said, "I know one thing for certain."

"What?" they all chimed simultaneously.

"This morning, I asked God to let me have a productive day. Whew. I ain't praying that anymore!" The roar of laughter shook my living room! They couldn't believe I had prayed for such a thing and then gone through such a frightful experience!

The next time I ask God for something, I will try to be more specific about my request. At least, He gave my neighbor lots of mercy! He gave my daddy deep insight about my illness – something the doctors could not do. And I began to realize that there were things I would have to learn slowly all over again during the next couple of years.

I still have a strong desire to see more of the world, even more of the USA. It may have to be on a ship or by train, but I **will** see this world one day soon!

There are many more stories I could add to this book, but they just "ain't fittin" to put in print!

Interesting Flight Tidbits

*Commute definition: Flying or driving from your home to your "Home base," in which your home can be anywhere in the world or the U.S. I flew with one pilot who commuted from Alaska. I also flew with a pilot who commuted from California to Baltimore. And I thought RDU was a long commute from Burlington, North Carolina.

**Crash Pad definition: A house where crewmembers would have a couple of hours to sleep after completing a two- or three-day trip at midnight or 1:00-2:00 a.m. Then they have to arise at 5:00 a.m. to shower and head back to the airport to catch the first flight home in the morning. I discovered it was interesting to use the word "crash" when associated with the airline industry, but quickly discovered why – we literally "crashed" upon completion of a trip.

When people from Rhode Island order, "Coffee regular," that means with cream, not black. Ask me how I found out? It only took one cup of black coffee for someone to quickly scold me, "Don't you know what regular coffee is?" After a bit of argument, they had regular coffee – their way – with cream!

When a passenger orders hot cocoa during a flight, you can bet the passengers in all the rows close by will smell the aroma, and all of them will add hot cocoa to their drink order. Always!

When I was a small girl, everyone dressed up in their Sunday clothes, the very best clothes they owned, to fly on an airplane. Not so anymore. It would require another book to describe fully the way people dress – and sometimes, barely dress to fly these days. We saw everything, sometimes much more than we cared to see.

During my first five years of flying, the airline did not allow pets even in a carrying cage or a ladies purse. Once, during pushback from the gate, as I made my safety walk down the aisle, checking to be sure all passengers had fastened their seat belts, as I approached the back section, I distinctly heard, "Meow." You can imagine my shock! I immediately asked my other crewmember at the back of the plane to come listen with me, and together we located the "hidden kitty" under the seat in front of the lady. We had to call the captain to pull back up to the gate to release the passenger and her kitty off the flight. It amazes me how she got through security and all three flight attendants hiding that cage with a silent kitty. Makes me wonder if she had drugged the kitty?

The airline never allowed passengers to bring their own "brown bag" on board. If there was to be a cocktail served, it was only airline liquor. During one flight, while I was still new on the job, we had served drinks and I was taking up trash. I caught a glimpse of a man hiding his large bottle of Crown Royal. My eyes got big as silver dollars when I spotted the pretty bottle. The passengers seated next to him probably thought I saw a snake. I may as well have. I wasted no time retrieving his bottle from him. He was so surprised at being caught and not allowed to use his own bottle of "liquid joy." The bottle was returned to the passenger upon landing. (I hope.)

The airline allowed passengers to have a "comfort animal" on board, as long as they had the appropriate paperwork from their doctor, signed, along with airline paperwork. I saw turtles, cats, and small doggies; once I saw a live sloth. It was amazing to watch the sloth move sooo slowly. He wrapped himself around the shoulder of the passenger.

Passengers used to ask, "Is there going to be a movie like on other airlines?" We usually told them, "Oh yes, just look out your window and watch, 'Gone with the Wind.' "

During one flight, I was taking up the trash, carrying a black plastic bag in one hand, and reaching for passengers' empty cups, napkins, etc. As

I approached the over-wing section of the plane, I focused so intently on picking up dropped articles of trash that I suddenly discovered I had extended my right hand to an improper place. A man seated in the aisle seat had his empty cup neatly situated in his crotch. Suddenly, aware of where my hand was reaching, I jerked it back, fully embarrassed at myself. The man looked up at me, broke into a huge smile, and said, "Honey, you can't blame a man for trying, can you?" We both chuckled, and he handed me his empty cup.

On a flight to West Palm Beach, Florida, we had 25 wheelchairs to preboard. It took quite a while to get that many wheelchair passengers on board. But a healing miracle occurred during flight. Upon landing in PBI (Palm Beach International), out of the twenty-five passengers, only four needed a wheelchair. The remaining wheelchair passengers walked off the plane, needing no assistance. Happens all the time!

It was always an honor for our flight crew to have military personnel on board. As we taxied to the gate after landing, the attendant working the front of the plane would make an announcement asking all passengers to kindly remain seated to allow the military passenger(s) to get off the plane first. This gesture was to make them aware that we honored their service to our country, but also to allow them to meet their loved ones as soon as possible. It never failed; each time the attendant announced this request, all loyal airline passengers not only remained seated, but they also applauded the military personnel in gratefulness for their service. It was always a touching and heartfelt moment with many smiles and teary eyes.

We are all aware of the Safety Demo, which is the announcement made during push back, just before take-off. Occasionally, just to break the silence and make everyone feel at ease, we would add the following announcement: "During the flight, if you have a sudden urge to smoke, we invite you to step out on our overhead wings. If you can light it, you may certainly smoke it!"

During the final descent of a particular flight, my crewmember made the following announcement: "Today we have a very special passenger aboard our flight. He is celebrating his 95th birthday. Please help us celebrate with a round of applause!" After the entire plane applauded, then the crewmember announced, "Thank you! And upon landing, you may shake our captain's hand and wish him a happy birthday as you exit our flight."

That's when the plane roared with laughter, knowing they had taken the joke. From that time forward, I couldn't resist emulating the joke on other flights. It always had the same result – a plane filled with applause and laughter!

Printed in the United States
By Bookmasters